The Kingdom of the
HORSE

The Kingdom of the
HORSE

Elwyn Hartley Edwards

CRESCENT BOOKS

New York

This 1991 edition published by Crescent Books,
distributed by Outlet Book Company, Inc.,
a Random House Company,
225 Park Avenue South,
New York, New York 10003.

ISBN 0-517-06553-3

87654321

CREDITS
Editor: Anne McDowall
Editorial assistant: Jenny Millington
Designers: Louise Bruce and Tim Scott
Colour reproductions: Scantrans Pte. Ltd.
Filmset: SX Composing Ltd.
Indexer: Stuart Craik
Printed and bound in Hong Kong

THE AUTHOR
Elwyn Hartley Edwards is one of the most prolific and authoritative equestrian
writers of the past 25 years. He is the author or editor of some 30 books and a
regular contributor to the equestrian press on a wide variety of subjects. For 18
years he edited the magazine *Riding* and was a prominent figure in the
development of the Riding Club movement, then for five years he was
Consultant Editor of *Horse and Hound*.
He is a regional chairman of the British Horse Society and President of two riding
clubs, judges horses, ponies and hounds, and has taken an active part in every
sort of horse sport. He lectures extensively on horse subjects, both in the UK and
overseas, and is a noted after-dinner speaker.

THE PHOTOGRAPHER
Most of the photographs in this book have been taken by and are the copyright of
Bob Langrish (others are credited on page 144).
Bob has been photographing the equestrian world for 18 years. His pictures
appear in more than 50 books and are regularly reproduced in equestrian
publications around the world.

CONTENTS

FOREWORD

The first association between man and horse may have begun a million or more years ago when men first assumed an upright stance and were learning how to hunt horses and other animals for food and other supports of the prehistoric life.

Much later, when Upright Man (*Homo erectus*) had become *Homo sapiens* – Wise Man, our still-primitive ancestors depicted the relationship between themselves and the horses they killed for meat in wonderfully vivid terms. The cave-drawings at Lascaux in France, for instance (and elsewhere in Europe and Africa, the work of artists living 20,000 years ago) were certainly a means of communication, telling other nomadic hunters of the presence of horse herds, but they had also a deeper significance beyond the purely secular. The cave drawings, created with such devotion, honoured the animals that provided the necessities of life. They are a reflection of the peculiar reverence accorded by the hunter to his quarry – one that has persisted in the beliefs of the shamanistic American Indian into our own times.

Today, modern men and women, despite their materialism, still maintain a special relationship with the animal that has partnered their progression from cave-dweller to traveller in space, regarding the horse with affection and admiration.

The Kingdom of the Horse is an appreciation of the remarkable animal race that underpins our history and is an expression of the unique position of 'the most noble of God's creatures' in human affairs. It is a tribute made, largely, in the modern equivalent of the art forms of early man – the coloured photograph, supported by an informative text.

This book tells the fascinating story of how the horse developed and how, through the intervention of men and women, breeds evolved that were best suited to particular purposes. It shows the huge variety of ways in which the horse has served us in war and peace and demonstrates the human reliance upon horse-power within the world's economy right up to the time when a man first set foot on the surface of the moon.

Today, when horses are no longer needed on the battlefield, to work the land or to transport goods, they still exist in huge numbers as a means of recreation transcending social barriers, and are still as necessary in our lives.

RIGHT: *Today, when it is possible for men and women to explore the worlds of outer space, the horse still has a place in our modern life.*
BELOW: *When man was still in his formative stage, the ancestors of these Exmoor Ponies had long been established on the earth.*

IN THE BEGINNING

The evolution of the species *Equus* began in recognizable form about 60 million years ago when the age of the Mammals succeeded that of the Reptiles, the latter becoming extinct as they ceased to be capable of adapting to the changing environment in which they lived.

The first ancestor of the horse was a primitive animal, classified mistakenly as *Hyracotherium* (viz. Hyrax, a genus of rabbit-like mammals) by the British anatomist Sir Richard Owen, after parts of a skull were discovered at Studd Hill in Kent during the 1920s. Scientists had discovered remarkably complete skeletons of this animal in rock structures of the Eocene Period when excavating in the southern parts of the USA as recently as 1867. Even more explicit remains were discovered in Wyoming in 1931, and this ancestor of the horse was reclassified as *Eohippus* (the Dawn Horse). From this small multi-toed creature, no bigger than a middle-sized dog, there emerged, about a million years ago, the forebear of the modern horse, the single-hoofed *Equus caballus*.

Eohippus, from which the progression to *Equus* can be traced on the American continent, derived from the extinct *Condylarth* group, the far-off ancestors of all hoofed creatures. The *Condylarth* had five-toed feet; *Eohippus* was equipped with four toes in front and three on the hindfeet. Behind the toes was a pad like those found on dogs and tapirs (the latter being a close relation of the horse). The pad suited the environment and assisted the animal in crossing soft, wet ground. It survives in the modern horse as the ergot, a superfluous horny growth on the back of the fetlock.

An average *Eohippus* would have weighed about 12lb (5.4kg) and would have stood some 14in (36cm) high at the shoulder. Its deer-like coat was probably blotched or spotted to provide a degree of camouflage in its forest-type habitat. The construction of the feet points to the environment being of the sort of soft soil occurring on the floors of semi-tropical jungle and around the edges of pools found in those areas. The eyes were placed centrally, limiting the lateral vision characteristic of the modern horse, and the short-crowned teeth were adapted to a diet of soft leaves found on low-growing shrubs. Another 30 million years were to elapse before the forest environment changed to grass-bearing open plains in the Miocene Period and compelled a further adaptation of the species.

RIGHT: *This mare and foal are the result of an evolution that began 60 million years ago on the North American continent.*
BELOW: *Mysterious Neolithic cave paintings have amazed generations of horsemen and scholars.*

The first horses

The prime factor governing evolution is the environment and the individual's ability to adapt to altered circumstance. A matter not so much of the survival of the fittest as of the survival of the best fitted. As the environment changed over millions of years, hundreds of strains of *Eohippus* became extinct – the mammoth *Megahippus*, for example.

Eohippus was followed by the three-toed *Mesohippus*, which in turn gave way to *Merychippus*, an animal that still had three toes but made increasing use of the central one and had a more advanced dental arrangement. *Merychippus* preceded *Pliohippus*, the first single-hoofed grazing animal equipped to survive on the virtually treeless plains, which had taken the place of the low jungles, and to be able to graze on the growth of wiry grasses. From this animal, which emerged about six million years ago, descended the true horse and also the zebras and asses.

This prototype for *Equus* had a ligament-sprung hoof; longer legs with flexing ligaments, which contributed to a running action similar to that of the modern horse; improved grazing dentition and greater lateral vision, which, together with a heightened sensibility and the ability to run from the threat of danger, made up the animal's defensive mechanism.

In the space of five million years the evolution to *Equus* was complete, and if the end product did not conform entirely to the modern horse, it was, nonetheless, recognizable as being of the same species.

From North America, the cradle of the equine race, *Equus* spread rapidly into South America (where previously there had been no horses), and over the existing land-bridges into Asia, Europe and Africa.

The Ice Age, extending up to 10,000 years ago, destroyed the feeding grounds as the ice packs engulfed the earth in successive waves and drove the horse population southwards. In the process the land-bridges joining the American continent to Europe and Asia disappeared,

LEFT: *The first founding father of the equine race was the Asiatic Wild Horse,* Equus Przewalskii Przewalskii Poliakov.

isolating the most important physical element in the history of equine development. At the end of the Ice Age horses inhabited Europe and the nearer parts of Asia, there were asses and zebras in the north and south of Africa respectively, and onagers (a type of wild ass) in the Middle East.

At about the same time, a phenomenon occurred which to this day remains one of the world's unsolved mysteries – the horse, together with the sloths and mastodons, became extinct on the continent that had watched over its evolution. No explanation can be found to account for the disappearance of these animals in North America; it might have been the result of some traumatic change in climate, or the onset of some fatal disease produced by a virulent insect, such as the African tsetse fly – no one knows. What is certain is that the equine species was not re-introduced to the continent until the sixteenth century, when Spanish *conquistadores* brought a complement of horses to Havana, Cuba, preparatory to the conquest of Mexico.

In the Old World, horses continued to develop according to the environment in which they lived. Temperate zones offering ample feed produced larger horses, the minerals and vitamins contained in the soil adding to their growth and strength. Where there was heavy rainfall and lush, succulent herbage, a heavier slow-moving animal evolved, as much disposed to browsing as grazing. Dry, desert-type environments produced lighter-boned specimens, swift moving but relatively small. Mountain regions and areas of climatic extremes supporting little plant growth encouraged the evolution of small, hardy ponies equipped for the rigours of their habitat.

Excluding the ass, zebra and onager, three clearly defined types evolved. There derived from them two principal horse types and two pony types, from which, it is held, all domestic stock descends.

The first of the founding fathers was the steppe horse – the Asiatic Wild Horse known scientifically as *Equus Przewalskii Przewalskii Poliakov*, the last name being that of the Polish colonel who discovered a wild herd in Mongolia in 1881. This primitive, dun horse with an upright mane is probably extinct in its original habitat, but is preserved in zoos worldwide.

TOP: *The lighter plateau horse, the Tarpan, evolved on the steppelands of eastern Europe.*

ABOVE: *The massive Ardennais has its origin in the slow-moving Forest or Diluvial horse.*

Further to the west was the plateau horse of eastern Europe and the Ukrainian steppes. It is called the Tarpan, or *Equus Przewalskii Gmelini Antonius*. It too has been hunted almost to extinction in the wild, but continues in a reconstituted environment in the famous Popielno herd of Poland.

The third horse, which is certainly extinct, was *Equus Przewalskii Silvaticus*, the Forest or Diluvial horse – a heavy, lumbersome specimen with broad, large feet, which lived in the wet, marshy lands of northern Europe.

There is a further wild horse to provide yet another unsolved mystery. It is the

Tundra horse, whose remains, along with those of the mammoths, have been found in north-east Siberia; otherwise it no longer exists in its wild form.

In the most general terms, the world's light horse population may be said to derive from Tarpan and Asiatic wild stocks, the former probably being at the root of the Arabian. The Forest Horse, possibly a variant of the Asiatic Wild Horse, is held to be the far-off ancestor of the heavy horse breeds of Europe. There is a suggestion that the Scandinavian pony stocks (which would include the Icelandic and Shetland ponies) could have been influenced by the mysterious Tundra Horse.

Domestic horses

Exactly when and where the horse joined the roll of domestic animals is unknown. There is a suggestion, based on a cave depiction showing a horse's head that appears to be fitted with a simple bridle, that it might have been as long ago as 12000 BC, which would place it level with the dog in the domestication charts. However, there is far more evidence to show that horses were domesticated by the nomadic steppe tribes in Eurasia some five to six thousand years ago at the end of the Neolithic period.

These people were of Aryan origin and their grazing grounds would have been the steppelands bordering the Black and Caspian Seas, for they were herders, or 'followers', of wild or semi-wild sheep and goats, and possibly of reindeer, too.

Initially they herded horses, using them as a supply of fresh meat on the hoof and milking the tamed mares. Quite quickly the horse became central to their lives, providing them not only with meat, milk and the heady fermented brew of the steppes, *kummis*, but with hides for clothes and shelter, and dung, which could be dried for their fires. Early in the association, particularly if the nomads had been reindeer people, horses would have been ridden and would have been used to carry the tribe's belongings or to drag them along on a simple *travois* (poles tied to each side of the horse which could be joined by thongs behind so as to form a platform).

The reason why nomadic herders should have switched from smaller animals to horses when they became available in sufficient numbers was that they were better equipped to forage for food in severe weather conditions. Unlike smaller animals they could manage in the snow and they were not tied to the reindeer's migratory cycle, which depended on the incidence of the 'reindeer moss' – its principal food.

Out of the high steppelands the domestic horse spread into central and western Europe, into and beyond the Caucasus, into Arabia and eastwards to China. From this time onwards a new factor was introduced into the equine evolutionary process as man began to use grain to feed the horses and bred them selectively to produce bigger, stronger and faster animals to suit particular purposes.

RIGHT: *These tough horsemen of Afghanistan are not unlike those early, nomadic peoples who were the first to maintain horse herds some 6,000 years ago on the steppelands of Eurasia.*
BELOW: *This cave drawing of a horse at Puerte Viesgo is much earlier than that – possibly around 12000 BC – and there is a suggestion of a rough bridle on the head.*

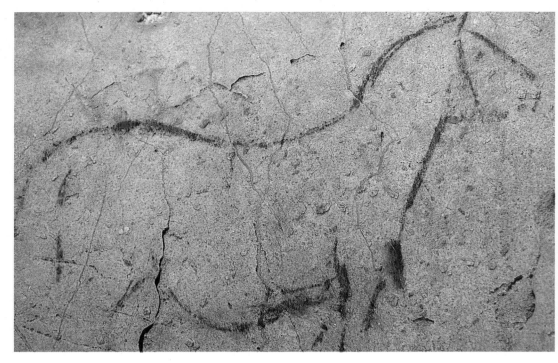

Horses at war and work

In the flat valley lands of the Middle Eastern countries, an area that for centuries was to be the cockpit of the known world, horses were used extensively in chariots, particularly, of course, for war, but also for peaceful transport. These early horses were too small to be ridden, but two or four hitched to a light chariot provided swift travel for two or three people. Great numbers of chariots were in use in the Middle East from 1600 BC, and when the

LEFT: *The war-chariot of Mesopotamia as it is depicted on the Standard of Ur (c.2500 BC).*
BELOW: *The Canadian Mounted Police, armed with lances, terminate their exciting displays with the traditional charge in line.*

Hittites defeated the forces of Rameses I of Egypt in the greatest chariot battle of antiquity at Kadesh in 1286 BC, they had 3,500 chariots in the field, supported by 17,000 foot soldiers.

Later civilizations, beginning with the Persians, developed the mounted cavalry arm as bigger horses became available and as it became necessary to move large bodies of troops over ground other than the flat deserts so suited to wheeled transport. Until the time of the Second World War, the armies of the world maintained a substantial horse complement. In 1939, for instance, the Polish army had 86,000 horses, while the German forces employed a total of some 1.2 million throughout the hostilities.

But there were also peaceful uses to which the horse could be put. The Romans, who were not great horsemen, preferring to employ auxiliary cavalry, were, nonetheless, pragmatic horse-breeders and organized studs for the production of everything from parade horses to pack animals. In antiquity the horse was too valuable and too much revered to be employed in any lowly task, oxen being used for agricultural purposes, as, indeed, they were in Europe for centuries. Only in the eighteenth and nineteenth centuries, as the heavy breeds became developed, did the horse win the battle of agricultural motive-power and come into general use.

Thereafter, horses were also used in vast quantities to provide transport and support the world's burgeoning industrial economies. London alone had a horse population of 300,000 in 1890, and thousands of horses were employed in the vast wheatlands of America and Canada, where 40-horse teams were used to draw the enormous combine harvesters.

From the beginning of time the horse has been immortalized in mythology and art. Horses were buried with kings, and sometimes white horses were offered to the gods as the ultimate sacrifice. To this day monarchs and captains use horses as the accompaniment to pomp and pageantry – and when they die their cortèges are followed by chargers carrying their reversed boots. Although horses are less often used for war and work today, they still retain a special place in custom and tradition.

BELOW: *Long before horses were used in agriculture, the land was ploughed by slow-moving teams of oxen. Only in the eighteenth and nineteenth centuries was the faster horse preferred and generally used.*

DRINKERS OF THE WIND

The Arabian Horse is the oldest breed in the world, the most pure and the most influential. In appearance it is uniquely beautiful and entirely distinctive.

The fixed type and character of the Arab is the result of centuries of careful selective breeding by the desert tribes, combined with the absence of any outside contaminative influence and an environment that produced horses with inherent qualities of stamina, hereditary soundness, conformational strength, courage and speed. Because of the exceptional purity of the desert strains, the Arab is a remarkably prepotent horse, passing on its qualities to its progeny and up-grading any other breed or type with which it is crossed, as well as increasing the size of the subsequent offspring.

The Arabian is regarded as the 'fountainhead' of the world's horse breeds,

for there is scarcely one that has not benefited in its development from this 'hot' Eastern blood. Even the heavy horse breeds, termed 'cold-bloods', have been influenced by Arab outcrosses and the world's fastest and most valuable horse, the Thoroughbred, derives directly from three prepotent Eastern foundation sires imported to England in the seventeenth and eighteenth centuries. All Thoroughbreds trace their descent from one of these three founding sires.

The term 'hot-blood' is not a reference to body temperature. It is applied to horses of Eastern origin that in days gone by might have been called variously Barb, Turk, Syrian etc. but that are now termed Arabian. Similarly, the Thoroughbred, originating with the Arab, is also considered to be a 'hot-blooded' horse. The heavy horse breeds of Europe are called 'cold-

bloods'. Crosses involving Thoroughbreds are described as half- or three-quarter-bred or, more usually today, go under the generic title of Warmblood.

The Arab, a horse more subject than any other to romantic myth and legend, is sometimes called Drinker of the Wind, a reference to the way in which the head is carried as a result of the angle at which it meets the neck. It is suggested that the high carriage of the head with its widely flared nostrils avoids the inhalation of dust, which would be inevitable at a lower level.

RIGHT: *The Arab's huge, expressive eyes, domed forehead, concave profile and small muzzle are unique features of the breed.*
BELOW: *A large herd of high-quality Russian-bred mares and foals. This distinctive type of Arab has been the principal up-grading influence in the Russian breeds.*

The origins and influence of the Arabian

The origins of the Arab are obscure; early art forms from the Nejd, Syria and Egypt depict small horses that are unmistakably Arab in character and they can be dated at around 2500-2000 BC. There is also evidence of a wild Oriental-type horse existing at about that time and before in southern Libya and western Iran, all round the cockpit of the Old World, in fact. It is certainly probable that the Caspian pony, discovered as recently as 1965 in the Caspian littoral, may have been a far-off prototype. Many authorities hold that a race of wild horses existed in central and southern Arabia, which in times past was 'a land of trees and rivers', possibly inhabiting the region as early as 5000 BC.

The Bedouin are the people most closely associated with the desert horse and, while they kept no written records, their traditional beliefs, passed on to succeeding generations by word of mouth, must be respected and taken seriously.

The Arab historian who recorded the history and pedigrees of the desert horses was El Kelbi. Writing in about AD 786, towards the end of the Muslim conquests, which had served to spread the influence of the Eastern horse through the Iberian Peninsula and from there deeper into central Europe, El Kelbi traced the development of the Arabian horses from around 3000 BC. His account begins with the mare Baz, captured by Bax the great-great-grandson of Noah in the deserts of Yemen where herds of wild horses were already established. How long they had been there can never be known, but it can be assumed that they had inhabited the area for some long period before Bax attempted their domestication.

As an historian, El Kelbi, like others of his race, was sometimes more allegorical than factual, but he produced highly detailed pedigrees of the Arabian horse families, each associated with one or other

LEFT: *In the Middle East, homeland of the desert horse, the indigenous stock is less than romantic. Though inherently tough, it is often stunted and degenerate in type.*

of the numerous Bedouin tribes. These families he traced to the progeny of the mare Baz and the stallion Hoshaba.

A thousand years later the Emir Abd-el-Kadr (1808-83) provided an explanation of the origins of the Arabian horse that went back to the ultimate point in time – that of the Creation. The Emir's explanation hardly accords with the Darwinian theory (Charles Darwin published *The Origin of the Species by Means of Natural Selection* in 1859) but it illustrates the affinity of the desert people with their horses and their regard for them within the Muslim life.

In a correspondence carried on over years with the French General, Melchior Daumas, who purchased horses for his government throughout Arabia and was the author of *Horses of the Sahara* (1850), the Emir answered his friend's question about the origin of the Arab horse in lyrical terms:

'Know then that amongst us it is accepted that God created the horse from the wind, as he created Adam from clay . . .'

God, wrote the Emir, condensed the south wind and from 'the stuff' presented to Him by the Angel Gabriel He made a 'brown bay or burnt chestnut (*koummite* – red mixed with black) saying, "I call you Horse (*frass*); I make you Arabian and I give you the chestnut colour of the ant; I have hung happiness from the forelock which hangs between your eyes; you shall be the lord (*sid*) of the other animals. Men shall follow you wherever you go; you shall be as good for pursuit as for flight; you shall fly without wings; riches shall be on your back and fortune shall come through your mediation." Then He put on the horse the mark of glory and happiness (*ghora*), a white mark in the middle of the forehead.'

Only the Arab horse could inspire that sort of tribute.

In the record of Abd-el-Kadr, the history of the Arabian horse was divided into four eras: Adam to Ishmael, the son of Abraham and first ancestor of the desert Bedouin, who it was held was the first man ever to ride a desert horse; Ishmael to Solomon; Solomon to Mohammed and then from the Prophet onwards.

RIGHT: *In contrast to the Arabian reality (shown left), nothing can exceed the glamour of the Arabian costume classes, which are a feature of American horse shows.*

ABOVE: *This charming Arab foal – an exceptionally good example of the breed – surveys the world with total confidence.*

RIGHT: *A unique feature of the Arab is the* jibbah *– the distinctive formation of the forehead, which bulges in a shield shape from between the ears down to the nasal bone.*

BELOW: *A striking Arab mare moving, characteristically, in perfect fluid balance, the tail held high like a banner.*

Ishmael was the fierce outcast, who obtained acceptance for himself and his followers through the possession of desert-bred horses as enduring and hardy as themselves and with which these early ancestors of the Bedouin people formed a unique relationship, caring for their horses as part of their families.

The desert tribes broke up after the death of Ishmael, but Solomon carried on the close association with the desert horse, keeping, we are told, no less than 40,000 chariot horses and between 1,200 and 2,000 riding horses in his stables.

But it is to the Prophet Mohammed that the world is indebted for the incalculable influence of the Arab horse. Mohammed was the unifier of the Arab people, uniting the tribes in a religious brotherhood and preaching a Holy War (*jihad*) which would ensure the spiritual extension of Islam. He was a shrewd politician and soldier as well as a religious leader, and fully appreciated that the furtherance of the Islamic faith would depend as much upon the swift, decisive movement of large mounted bodies as upon religious zeal. Central to that practical concept was the possession of horses in sufficient numbers and of exceptional quality.

The astute Mohammed incorporated the management and well-being of the horse as a tenet of the faith, proclaiming the horse in the Koran as 'the supreme blessing' and its care a religious duty which, if observed, would ensure the delights of Paradise for the fortunate owner. 'A horse scrupulously bred for the Holy War will save his master from the fire on the Day of Resurrection', and then, with an eye on the material appeal, 'Happiness in this world, *rich booty* and eternal reward are attached to the horse's forelock.' In this manner the Prophet exhorted his followers to 'love horses and look after them.' It was heady stuff and a powerful incentive to fanatical warriors who welcomed death in battle as a certain passport to the eternal joys of Paradise, and it led to a breed of horses that, because of its singular qualities, would in time govern the development of the world's horse population for hundreds of years.

The Bedouin horses lived near or within the black tents of their masters. In a land with little or no edible herbage they were hand-fed with grain, milk, dates and, when they were available, balls of fish and cooked meat. In circumstances of such close and caring contact, the Arab horse became naturally docile and gentle and developed a very unusual intelligence. The sale of horses to infidels was prohibited and breeding was carefully selective, the purity of the recognized strains being jealously preserved. It was, indeed, customary for centuries for the mating of a mare and the subsequent foaling to be witnessed by a committee of selected tribal elders.

After the death of Mohammed in AD 632, the warriors of Islam burst out of their desert lands to plant the green standards of the moslem faith up to the walls of China on the one hand, and as far as the ramparts of Europe on the other.

In the process of these embracing conquests, the blood of the supreme Arabian horse permeated the greater part of the world's equine races, culminating, in the late seventeenth and the eighteenth centuries, in the emergence of the world's super-horse, the Thoroughbred, an animal that in size, speed and performance ability would outstrip its progenitor. Nonetheless, the Thoroughbred does not approach the Arab either in terms of endurance or in the inherited soundness of constitution.

The ancestry of the Arabian

The principal strains recognized by the desert tribes and that are still generally acknowledged as being of special value are: Seglawi, Hadban, Munaghi, Nowak, Dahman, Krush, Abeyan, Wadnan, Jilfan, Jellabi and Hamdani.

Inevitably in any study of the Arabian horse we come up against the *Khamsa*, a corporate word for what are considered the five foundation strains. The first and the oldest is Kehilan, meaning 'pure-bred' but always qualified by the word Ajuz (i.e.

LEFT: *A fiery Arab stallion expresses the joy of living in an exuberant rear, which in no way disturbs the composure of his rider.*
BELOW: *A poem in motion. There is a wonderful freedom in the floating movement of this beautiful Arabian horse.*

Kehilan Ajuz), which is the name of a mare from the line of Baz and the stallion Zad er Rakib – a horse given to the tribe of Ben Zad by King Solomon himself in about 1000 BC. The second is Seglawi, the pure strain being Seglawi Jedran, then Abeyan, Hadban and Hamdani. Munaghi, the racing strain, and the others are excluded from the elite foundation group.

Some authorities reject the Khamsa and its related legends as 'a pious fairy tale' but in practical terms it still finds acceptance.

The Arab story has it that when God made a gift of 100 horses to Ishmael, the latter carried out a sort of selection test. He withheld water from the horses for eight days and then loosed the herd on the sea shore. All rushed to drink the salt water except the mare Ajuz. She stood by the water's edge and out of the sea arose a great stallion who mated with her. In time she gave birth to the colt called Kehilan Ajuz.

Another version has the Prophet himself releasing a thirsty herd to water and then

calling them back. Only five mares obeyed the call. They became the five founding dams of the Khamsa and the Prophet signified their special worth by placing his thumb on their necks. The imprint left a whorl of hair and that mark, which some horses still bear today, is called the Prophet's Thumbmark, and is thought to be possessed by horses of particular merit.

Certainly these are fairy tales; incontestable, however, are the numerous records of the Arab's endurance and stamina – feats that would have been seen as commonplace by the desert tribes.

There is the story of Si-ben-Zyam, who rode his father's favourite mare to Algiers to prevent her requisition by the Turks. He rode through the night, stopping only to allow the mare to drink and once for a short rest. The distance from their home to Leghrouat was 240 miles (380 km) and the journey was completed in 24 hours, with the mare still in fit condition to have carried on if it had been necessary.

Arabian racehorses

Arab races were held not so much over a set distance as by days – three days being usual.

One famous and versatile Arab horse was Maidan, born in the Nejd in 1869 and sold in Bombay two years later. His owner, Captain Johnstone, raced him successfully on the flat and over fences, and won with him the Blue Riband of that demanding sport of pig-sticking, the Kadir Cup. His next owner, Colonel Brownlow, who weighed between 15 and 16 stones (95 and 100kg) continued to race him, and then took him off to the Afghan campaign of 1879-80 as his charger, during which the pair made many fatiguing forced marches.

Maidan returned to Europe in the ownership of Captain Vesey, stopping off at Suez to take part in the relief of Suakin, and in conditions of great heat made the journey from Port Said to Massawa and back, a distance of 866 miles (1,400km) as the crow flies but longer on the ground.

Continuing the journey home, Maidan paused at Marseilles to race over the banks of the Pau country. At 20 years of age in England he won three point-to-point races against Thoroughbreds and won a three-mile steeplechase when he was 22. Unhappily, he broke a leg during the following year and had to be destroyed, but his blood still figures in the pedigrees of many modern Arabians.

The greatest achievement of the Arab, however, is the English Thoroughbred, which owes its existence to three imported stallions crossed with the native running stock, which itself had acquired a strong Eastern influence over a long period.

The first was the Byerley Turk, captured at the Battle of Buda in Hungary and subsequently ridden by his owner, Colonel Byerley at the Battle of the Boyne in 1690. He founded the first of the four direct male lines of the modern Thoroughbred, that of Herod; and Herod's son, Highflyer, was responsible for the second line. The third, that of one of the greatest racehorses of all time, Eclipse, was founded by the Darley Arabian, imported from Aleppo in 1704, while the Matchem line was the responsibility of the Godolphin Arabian, born in the Yemen in 1724 and brought to England in 1729.

The modern Arabian

The Arab is not a big horse, the usual height being around 14.3 hands high (the height of a horse is measured in 'hands', one hand equalling 4in/10 cm). The Arab's conformation, however, is unmistakable, although there are minor differences of type between a Polish-bred Arab and an Egyptian, for example. The outline of the Arab in motion, head held high with the tail arched upwards like a banner, is largely a result of the unique skeletal conformation, which differs from that of other horses. The Arab has 17 ribs, five lumbar bones and 16 tail vertebrae in comparison with the 18-6-18 formation in other horses.

The head of the Arab is most distinctive. It is short, very refined, and covered with a thin skin through which the veins are clearly visible. The face is pronouncedly dished in profile, the muzzle being tapered and so small that it fits into a half-cupped hand. The texture of the skin is especially soft and the hair is fine and silky – far more so than in other breeds. As for the eyes, set on a broad forehead, they dominate the outlook, being exceptionally large. The horse's action is as unique as its appearance – the horse floating as though it were on springs. 'Nature, when she made the Arab, made no mistake.'

LEFT: *The Arab is not as fast as the Thoroughbred, but racing confined to Arabs is a growing sport and just as exciting.*

BELOW: *Nothing can approach the pure-bred Arab's nobility of outlook. No horse is more beautiful and few are more intelligent.*

ANCIENT BREEDS

It is accepted that the Arabian horse is the most ancient of all breeds, but there are others almost as old, and some that seem to have largely avoided the all-pervasive influence of the hot-blooded desert horse. These are the horses and ponies that appear to trace their descent from primitive prehistoric stock – the Asiatic Wild Horse, for instance, and the Tarpan – and to have maintained a separate identity.

Many of the European breeds are the creations of the eighteenth and nineteenth centuries, bred at the great studs of Europe, such as the impressive establishments of the vast Austro-Hungarian Empire. Most of them were formed on the basis of Spanish blood, which today is interpreted as Andalucian. Spanish horses were regarded as the supreme riding horses of the seventeenth and eighteenth centuries. They were the favoured mounts of kings and generals, and they provided the dominant breeding influence for over 200 years, eclipsing even that of the less available Arab. Lipizzaners, Kladrubers, Frederiksborgs, Cleveland Bays and Irish Draughts all owe something to the Spanish horse, while the American breeds, formed over a brief two centuries, are for the most part based firmly on Spanish blood.

In fact, of course, the Andalucian or Spanish horse can be regarded as the third influence in the formation of most of the world's breeds. The second after the Arab was the Barb of North Africa, a horse which was largely responsible for the Andalucian. The latter came about as a result of Barb horses, brought to the Iberian Peninsula during the Muslim, or Moorish, occupation, being crossed with the indigenous and near-primitive stock.

The Barb is a desert hot-blood horse, possibly related to the Arab but quite unlike it in appearance, although its influence, if less recognized, has been very great. There is a theory that the Barb may have constituted an isolated pocket of wild horses on the fertile Moroccan coastal strip which escaped the ravages of the Ice Age, thus preserving another prepotent gene bank.

RIGHT: *The splendid Spanish horse we now call Andalucian had a dominant influence on the world horse population for over two centuries.*
BELOW: *Less noble in appearance but of even greater importance is the North African Barb, the progenitor of the Spanish horse.*

The Camargue

The Camargue horse was without doubt influenced by the Barb horses brought to its watery habitat in the Rhône delta of southern France by the Moorish invaders in the seventh and eighth centuries. Those horses bred with the indigenous stock of the area, and the isolation of the inhospitable Camargue has since ensured that the half-wild herds of white horses, the *manades*, have been untouched by outside influences.

There are paintings of horses on the cave walls at Lascaux that very much resemble the modern Camargue, and the much older remains of prehistoric horses of similar proportions, which were discovered at Solutré in the last century, may well be those of the breed's ancestors.

The harsh environment of the Carmargue swamplands is dominated by the cutting *mistral*, the salt-laden wind which blows interminably over the stunted plant growth. In the summer the sun is fierce and drying, and at other times the desolate land, rich only in its abundant wild life, is covered with an icy sheet of salt water. This has played an obvious part in the independent character of the Camargue pony, which is tough enough to exist on a diet foraged from the reed beds. There is, nonetheless, the influence of the vigorous primitive gene. It is apparent in the courage of the Camargue, and in the endless reserves of stamina and endurance that make it the chosen mount of the Camargue cowboys, the *gardiens*, in their contact with the ferocious black bulls who share this stark delta. It is revealed, too, in the pony's appearance. Standing about 14 hands high, the Camargue is by no means an exemplary pattern of equine conformation. It has a heavy, primitive head, a short neck, upright shoulders and a low-set tail in downward sloping quarters. In fact, it is not unlike the early North African horses before the refining introduction of Arab blood. For all that, this 'horse of the sea' is fiery, agile and sure-footed, moving with an action that is peculiarly its own. It has a very long high-stepping walk, a short, stilted trot, which is uncomfortable and seldom employed, but an amazingly free canter and gallop.

Further to the East there are two more breeds as unique as the Camargue.

The Caspian

The Caspian pony, postulated now as part of the Arab progression, relates, like all equines, to one of the four types which had evolved prior to domestication. The scientists, whose researches led them to conclude that there were such sub-types deriving from the earliest primitives, defined two pony and two horse types.

LEFT: *The Camargue horse in its watery environment in France's Rhône delta. The harsh habitat has produced a hardy, vigorous horse of independent character.*
BELOW: *The Caspian pony, in reality a small horse, is held to have been the prototype for the illustrious Arabian.*

Horse Type 4, to which the Caspian is closest, was the smallest of all, perhaps not more than nine hands high, but it was the most refined. It was light of limb with a neat head, concave profile and a high-set tail. Its habitat was Western Asia. It was originally classed as a horse, albeit in miniature, because it had horse characteristics and proportions rather than those of a pony.

The trilingual seal of Darius the Great (c. 500 BC) shows very small horses of this sort drawing a chariot, and almost identical animals appear on Egyptian reliefs of 1,000 years before. No-one had ever seen such horses in the flesh until Mrs Louise L. Firouz discovered a small herd of just such small equines at Amol, in the area of the Caspian Sea, as recently as 1965.

Because of its size (10-12 hands high and so bigger than Horse Type 4) the Caspian is now called a pony. It is distinctive because as well as the horse proportions, it has different physical characteristics to other equines, some of which appear in prehistoric remains. It has, for instance, an extra molar in the upper jaw; the scapula (shoulder-blade) is of a different shape, and there is a peculiar formation of the parietal bones of the head, giving the forehead a vaulted shape. The ears are very short, the eyes large and the skin exceptionally fine. It has a natural floating action, and is said to be able to keep pace with a horse at all gaits other than the gallop.

There are now studs in Iran and thriving Caspian societies in Britain, America, Australia and New Zealand.

The Akhal-Teke

In the oases of the Turkmenistan desert, on the northern border of Iran, one of the world's most distinctive and unusual horses is to be found. This is the Akhal-Teke, a true desert horse which approximates almost exactly to Horse Type 3, defined as being a bigger horse, about 14.3 hands high, long and narrow in the body, goose-rumped, with a long neck and the long, mobile ears associated with desert animals. It was an inhabitant of Central Asia and peculiarly resistant to heat. The description, allowing for an increase in height to about 15.2-15.3 hands fits the unprepossessing modern Akhal-Teke very accurately.

Russian authorities claim that the breed has been kept pure for 3,000 years, and that it has no connection with the ancient Persian, Assyrian or, indeed, the Arabian horse. The argument is based on the isolated geographical position of the Turkmene oases which, it is said, ensured that no outside crosses could be introduced. Also, like the Bedouin, the ancient Turkmene warriors preserved their horses' blood lines with a rare dedication, passing down pedigrees by word of mouth from generation to generation.

Archaeological discoveries provide every reason to suppose that a race of horses, virtually identical in character to the modern Akhal-Teke, did exist in Turkmenistan over 3,000 years ago, but otherwise the official Russian view is not acceptable to western historians. Inevitably, in that long space of time, there was a cross-fertilization of cultures, people and horses as the Turkmens were involved in campaigns outside their desert home. It seems certain that the Akhal-Teke was influenced by neighbouring Persian horses, and by the Arabian. In fact, the Akhal-Teke bears a resemblance to the old type of Munaghi Arab, the racing strain, which was not always so typical of the breed, particularly in relation to its straight profile.

The character of this strange horse, however, is the result of its environment and the hard ascetic lifestyle of the Turkmens. The horses, like the men, were bred to withstand conditions of great heat and privation, and the exigencies imposed by warfare and raiding produced a fast horse of great endurance.

These horses were never stabled. They stood tethered in the mid-day heat, and in the bitter desert nights were wrapped in massive felt blankets. They carried not an ounce of surplus fat, an ideal condition for racing, a sport to which the Turkmens are passionately addicted. When being trained to race, they were fed, much like the horses of the Bedouin, on a high-protein diet of dry lucerne (when available), pellets of mutton fat, eggs, a little barley and *quatlame* – a cake of fried dough.

The long-distance records set by the Akhal-Teke horses are phenomenal. In 1935, for instance, a group of Akhal-Teke horses completed a ride from Ashkabad to Moscow, a distance of 2,580 miles (4,150 km), in 84 days. A quarter of the journey was over desert, much of it without water. The feat has never been equalled, although horses of the breed still make such journeys.

A particular feature of the breed, common to desert-bred horses, is the peculiar metallic sheen on the fine coat. Manes and tails are sparse and wispy and the skin exceptionally thin. The horse's conformation could not be expected to meet with approval by European standards but very few horses, if any, could compete with the Akhal-Teke on its home ground.

RIGHT: *The metallic sheen on the fine coat is typical of the Akhal-Teke and is common to many desert-bred horses.*
BELOW: *A herd of modern-day Akhal-Teke enjoying the plant growth of a rough pasture.*

The Yakut

Far to the north of the Turkmene deserts, in climatic conditions opposite to those endured by the Akhal-Teke, there is a breed of pony that is virtually prehistoric in character. It is the Yakut of the Yakut Autonomous Republic, which extends beyond the Arctic Circle and where winter temperatures are below those at the North Pole. Scientists believe that the Yakut ponies are the direct descendants of the prehistoric strain, the Tundra Horse. Certainly the appearance of the Yakut is unmistakably primitive. Not surprisingly, since these ponies live in the open in below-freezing conditions for much of the year, they grow long, thick manes and tails, and coats that can measure as much as six inches (15cm) in length. The colours are often of the primitive dun shades, and the animals, like much wild stock, turn white in winter. Zebra marks on the legs, a latticed pattern on the shoulder and dorsal stripes are all indicative of a primitive origin, confirmed by the coarseness of the head.

Nonetheless, the Yakut ponies are much valued and are used as pack animals, in harness and under saddle, as well as for meat. Working animals and mares are fed a little in hard weather, and in the summer, when the herds are so plagued by mosquitos that they cannot graze, smoke fires are lit to protect them from the insects.

BELOW: *One of the hardiest equines in the world, and the one most resistant to cold, is the primitive, almost prehistoric Yakut.*

The Fjord Pony

The Norwegian Fjord is a very much more attractive pony, found in a variety of types throughout Scandinavia and beyond. It is, nonetheless, indigenous to Norway and of all the modern breeds bears the closest resemblance to the Asiatic Wild Horse, even though it has been much refined by selective breeding. It retains all the primitive vigour as well as the characteristic dun colour, with dorsal stripes and sometimes zebra bars on the legs. Additionally it has the erect, coarse mane that is a feature of the primitive equine.

The mane of the Fjord pony, if left untended, would, in fact, grow as long as that of other breeds, although it would retain its harsh, bristle-like quality. By tradition, dating back to the Viking age, the mane is carefully hogged (roached) so that the black hairs at its centre stand above the rest. The whole is cut in a crescent shape to accentuate the crest of the neck, exactly as can be seen in the rune-stone carvings of the Vikings. This was, indeed, the horse of the Vikings, which was carried in their longboats and was often used in the popular sport of horse-fighting.

The Fjord is very much a working horse, still taking the place of the tractor on the remote mountain homesteads of its native land. It is also used as a pack horse, as well as for riding and driving.

BELOW: *The predominantly dun Norwegian Fjord – the horse of the Viking warriors – is very similar to the Asiatic Wild Horse.*

The Icelandic Horse

It was the Norsemen who settled in the volcanic North Atlantic island that we know as Iceland between AD 860 and 935, bringing with them their sturdy horses, who were responsible for the Icelandic breed.

These horses, of essentially primitive origin, played a part in the development of the British native breeds, and in Iceland they became integral to the life of the inhabitants. There is still a strong horse-culture on this island where horses almost equal the human population in number.

Remarkably, the horses, for they are always termed as such even though they stand no more than 13.2 hands high, have not changed essentially in over 1,000 years, although they have been bred selectively for centuries. Once, about 1,000 years ago, there was an abortive attempt to introduce Eastern blood. It failed so disastrously that in AD 930 the Icelandic Althing, the world's oldest parliament, prohibited the import of horses, which accounts for the extreme purity of the breed.

Selective breeding takes account of the five gaits peculiar to the Icelandic horse, and also the coat colour. The Icelandic breed has no less than fifteen basic types and colour combinations, the wide range being a source of pride among the islanders.

The gaits are the walk (*fetgangur*) used under pack; trot (*brokk*) for crossing rough country; gallop (*stökk*), and the ancient pacing gait (*skeid*) for covering short distances at speed. Finally, there is the renowned *tolt*, the rapid, four-beat, running walk.

The Icelandic horse is quite capable of carrying a grown man over long distances, and horse sports, particularly racing, are enormously popular, but otherwise the horses carry out every sort of work in a land where few made-up roads exist.

LEFT: *The Icelandic Horse, which remains integral to the conomy and traditions of Iceland. Essentially, this selectively bred horse has not changed in over 1,000 years.*
RIGHT: *The Friesian horse of Holland, where it is highly regarded, contributed to the development of horse breeds far outside its homeland, including England's Dales and Fells ponies and its Shire horse.*

The Friesian

One of the most interesting and influential of Europe's cold-blood breeds is the Friesian, a descendant of the ancient Forest Horse. It has been bred for centuries on Friesland in northern Holland and occupies an important place in equine history.

It was known to the Romans as an excellent all-round work horse of exceptional ugliness. Its looks were improved when it became the war-horse of the Friesian and German knights during the Crusades and benefited from Eastern and Spanish blood. It was, indeed, the most practical horse for that purpose, for it was sound, enduring, up to weight and the cheapest of all to keep.

Germany's great Oldenburg breed was founded on the Friesian horse, which itself became a notable harness horse that would also go under saddle and work on the farm.

The Friesian also played its part in the development of England's Dales and Fell Ponies when the Frieslanders came to the north of England, with their black horses, as flank-guards for the Roman legions. It made a major contribution, with the big horses of Flanders, to the Great Horse of England, which later became the English Black and then the majestic Shire.

The circus appreciated these agile, good-natured, jet-black horses for every sort of equestrian act and their natural presence, as well as their colour, assured them a role as the funeral horse *par excellence* well into the twentieth century.

HORSES AT WORK

The variety of tasks undertaken by horses over some 6,000 years is enormous and sometimes surprising.

Three hundred years before the Christian era, the Persian kings had established an empire stretching from Egypt to Asia Minor and from India to the Greek Islands. To hold together an empire of this magnitude there had to be a comprehensive system of communication. The Persians built roads to create just such a system, and it was a remarkably efficient one. It was possible, by using relays of horses, for 1,500 miles (2,400km) to be covered in seven to 14 days and the horses – the Niseans – used were the pride of the ancient world and central to the rise of the Persian Empire. They were bred in north-west Iran and were an amalgam of Eastern blood with possible

outcrosses to the Asiatic Wild Horse and, since the stirrup had yet to be invented, they were probably comfortable pacing horses, moving the legs in lateral pairs.

The Mongols of Genghis Khan operated a strikingly similar system – the Yam – 1,800 years later with relays of messengers on hardy Mongolian ponies riding 150 miles (242km) a day to cover the whole of the known world.

Some 600 years later, in April 1860, William H. Russell, 'the Napoleon of the Plains', inaugurated the American Pony Express to carry the mail through hostile Indian country between Missouri and San Francisco. The route was from St. Joseph, Missouri, through Kansas, Nebraska, Colorado, Wyoming, Utah and Nevada to Sacramento. The distance was 1,966 miles

(3,614km), and each rider, who it was stipulated should be 'skinny, wiry, not over 18' and 'preferably an orphan', rode 60 miles (96km) as fast as his pony could lay feet to the ground. The journey was covered, using 400 ponies, in ten days.

Without the horse it would have been impossible for the American West to be won, and long after the pioneer days the American economy depended on the horse. In fact by 1914 America had upwards of twenty-five million horses.

RIGHT: *The Whitbread Shires, which still deliver beer in the City of London, are famous throughout Great Britain.*
BELOW: *Throughout the Soviet Union, and in much of eastern Europe, the horse is still an essential element in the rural economy.*

Horses and the mail

In Europe, relatively sophisticated systems of communication operated in the eighteenth and nineteenth centuries, particularly in Britain. At the end of the eighteenth century, mail was carried by post boys, often poorly mounted on rough-actioned horses. To avoid the discomfort of uneven paces, they learnt and practised the rising trot, the seat being raised from the saddle at alternate strides. This became known as 'posting' to the trot, and on the European mainland was for long dubbed the 'English trot'. Later, mail carts, able to carry parcels as well as letters, were added to the service, and for express mail one could use the faster but expensive post-chaise.

The basis of the present postal system in Britain, which became the pattern for so many others, was the service initiated in 1784 by John Palmer, the Postmaster General, who was also a coaching enthusiast. It depended upon a system of good roads, but in 1780 there were only 5,000 miles (8,000km) of road, which was no increase on the number of surfaced *via strata* provided in Roman Britain. By 1830, when the short-lived coaching era was well under way, that figure had increased to 20,000 miles, (32,000km) largely because of two Scotsmen, Thomas Telford, the builder of bridges and roads, and John MacAdam, immortalized by the method of surfacing known as 'macadam' and 'tarmacadam'.

Critical, of course, to the success of the operation was the availability of suitable horses. In this respect, Britain had the advantage of the Thoroughbred horse, which by 1770 was firmly established. If anything, the situation in the racing market was one of over-production, which gave rise to a surplus of animals to supply harness teams. Horses of this quality, and the Cleveland Bay Thoroughbred cross called the Yorkshire Coach Horse, could, given light vehicles and sound road surfaces, attain high speeds over long distances when used in relay.

Palmer's first mail coach ran from Bristol to London, via Bath, on 2 August 1784. Travelling through the night, it completed the journey in 15 hours at an average 12 mph (19 kph), arriving at the General Post Office in London exactly on schedule at eight o'clock the next morning. The modern postal system is not more efficient and sometimes less so.

The mail coaches encouraged private operators to run passenger coaches operating to the same high standards, and between 1825-45, which was the 'golden age' of coaching, Britain achieved a system of transport that was 'the wonder of the age and the envy of Europe.'

LEFT: *A pair of Friesian horses that have achieved a place in high society; they draw the delivery van of Harrods, one of the world's most famous stores.*
RIGHT: *The Shire horses, which still make daily beer deliveries in London, are one of the city's most popular sights.*
BELOW: *Until about the middle of this century, most of Britain's milk was delivered by carts drawn by Welsh Cobs like these.*

Horse-power in industry

It was horse-power that provided the means by which strong foundations were laid for the modern communication networks, and when the railways put an end to the magnificent era of the road coach, the Industrial Revolution they heralded was still dependent upon the efforts of horses. In fact, the railways, servicing the huge increase in manufacturing, were a positive incentive to the employment of horses.

Goods and raw materials, coal to feed the furnaces and foodstuffs for city dwellers all had to be moved to and from railheads; an increasing number of passengers required transport, and the whole smoke-wreathed structure was supported by horses. Indeed, the use of working horses for industrial and urban deliveries continued beyond the Second World War.

For well over a century the railway companies were the biggest employers and owners of horses. At the turn of the century more horses were working in the towns of Britain than on the land, and in the 1890s there were 300,000 horses on the streets of London alone.

Horses were much used in the goods yards for the shunting of rolling stock, and did the work more efficiently and cheaply than steam engines. The last horse regularly employed in shunting was stationed at Newmarket, the headquarters of the racing industry in England. He moved the horse-boxes in the sidings, the transportation of horses by rail then being the rule rather than the exception, and he was not retired from service until 1967.

The first railway horses were those hauling passenger coaches over short distances on tramways. This system preceded the steam engine, and was first used by the Surrey Iron Railway, which ran a horse-drawn service between Wandsworth and Croydon in 1803. It survived for an extraordinarily long time. The Fintona branch line in Northern Ireland was using horse-drawn passenger coaches until 1957.

Elsewhere in Europe the horse railway survived even longer. One of the most famous horse lines connected the city of Linz in upper Austria with Budweis in Bohemia. The total length of track was 124 miles (200km) and in its heyday in the late

1800s it transported some 150,000 passengers a year and 100,000 tons of freight, mostly salt from the Saltzkammergut area to Bohemia. The journey took 14 hours.

The principal source of power for the railways and much of the manufacturing industry was coal, even though the measure of power was expressed, as it is today, in terms of 'horse-power'. (One horse power is the force required to raise 550lb one foot (830kg one metre) in one second.)

Horses worked at the pitheads, turning the windlass of the hoist, as well as drawing coal wagons. And, of course, there were the pit ponies working and living underground. There was a substantial trade with the mines for Shetland and Welsh ponies. British mines employed ponies in the larger pits up to 1972, but in smaller, privately owned mines in south Wales ponies are still used. Horse mills, often worked by blind horses, were operated where wind- and water-mills were impractical, and a lot of farm machinery, root choppers, grist mills and so on, were horse-powered.

Horses also worked on the comprehensive network of waterways comprising the canal system, which had been established for the transportation of goods early in the eighteenth century. Both freight and passengers were carried in horse-drawn barges, and the general use of barge-horses survived into the late 1950s, while a few are still employed in the holiday industry.

There was no specific breed of barge horse. For the most part the 'boaters' were a light draught type of Irish extraction, or smaller types deriving from the accepted heavy draught breeds. Because of the height of the bridges they could not be much over 15.2 hands high, but strength was a paramount consideration, for the loads they hauled could amount to more than 60 tons. It was estimated that one horse and three men could move as much by barge as 60 horses and 10 men could haul in a wagon on the roadways. The usual speed of travel was a steady 2mph (3.2kph), but, by employing relays of trotting horses on short stages, 50-60 miles (80-90km) could be covered in a day.

LEFT: *The Shire horse played an important part in the system of British agriculture until the Second World War.*

An even quicker form of transport was provided by the high-speed fly boat, the equivalent of the twentieth century hydrofoil. It was a shallow craft, drawing not more than 18 inches (46cm) of water, and it was towed by two horses, one hitched to the bow and the other to the stern. Sometimes the rear horse was ridden by a postillion who controlled the lead horse with his whip and voice, and on at least one waterway, the Grand Union, the postillion rode the lead horse. Once the boat got under way, the horses maintained a steady canter which caused the bow to lift and the boat to plane over the water. Using relays of horses over three to five mile (5-8km) stages, these boats could average speeds of 10-12 mph (16-19 kph).

Until the nineteenth century, Britain also had a transport network made up of pack trails. Elsewhere in the world, in regions where the terrain was mountainous and there were no roadways as such, there was far more reliance upon the extensive use of pack animals.

BELOW: *Farm horses started their working day at first light, returning to their stables in mid-afternoon. These big Shires, standing 17 hands high, originated in England's Midland Counties.*

In the more remote Asian republics of the USSR, transport is still largely dependent upon sure-footed pack ponies. In the Carpathian mountain regions, the tough Hucul pony carries heavy loads over difficult mountain paths covered in snow and ice, while the Bosnian, the primitive little mountain horse of Macedonia, is selectively bred to carry pack loads. Stallions must prove their suitability by packing a 2cwt (100kg) load over 10 mountainous miles. Most of them complete the distance in not much more than an hour and a quarter.

In Tibet and throughout the Himalaya range, as, indeed, throughout the East, incredibly small ponies, often exhibiting every sort of conformational fault, carry enormous loads in comparison with their size, and do so without the supplementary feeding considered necessary in the West.

The weights that can be carried by ponies are, indeed, considerable. In Britain, where both the Dales and Fell ponies were used in

pack trains to cart lead from the hill mines to the Tyneside ports, a pack load was fixed at 224lb (101kg) and the ponies averaged 240 miles (386km) per week over difficult, mountainous ground. Another notable English breed that began as a pack-horse is the impressive Cleveland Bay, which derived from the Chapman horse of north-east England, a pack-horse that carried the wares of the travelling salesmen (the chapmen), as well as transporting minerals from the Cleveland mines to the sea.

Without doubt, however, it is the mule that is the supreme pack animal. It is not only incredibly tough but it is also claimed to be 25 per cent more powerful than any other equine in relation to its size. Furthermore, it has the ideal back conformation to carry a pack saddle, the mule's back being long and virtually straight from withers to croup. Animal transport companies are still a feature of twentieth century armies, and in India they still carry the guns of the mountain artillery batteries.

BELOW: *America can boast the world's largest mule population. This is a mammoth mule, bred from a Belgian Heavy Draught mare.*
BOTTOM: *In Third World countries, such as Guatemala, ponies like this one do every kind of work, often carrying extraordinarily heavy loads in relation to their size.*

Working horses today

Most armies continue to maintain mounted troops for ceremonial purposes and some still make use of horses operationally. Both China and Russia have mounted divisions on their mountainous borders, the former using the hardy Mongolian pony. India also has a mounted regiment, which patrols the long border with Pakistan, as well as the much larger Border Security Force, a mounted police force with direct responsibility for the frontier.

The majority of police forces throughout the world have a mounted branch, and it has been proved time and time again that mounted policemen riding carefully trained horses constitute the best form of crowd control and are an effective means of patrolling city streets.

Up to 1940, thousands of heavy horses were working in agriculture, 650,000 in Britain alone, and there were many more in America, a country which had the largest mule population in the world. In 1920 it numbered an astonishing 5,432,000, and the mule was much appreciated on account of its hardiness and longevity, as well as because it could be kept more easily and more cheaply than a horse. Even now, America produces some of the finest mules in the world. At the Kentucky Horse Park, Lexington, a uniquely comprehensive complex devoted to the horse in all its aspects, there is, for instance, a complement of 'mammoth' mules bred from the Horse Park's splendid Belgian Heavy Draught mares. These mules, some of them distinctively chestnut coloured like their dams, are one of the Park's many attractions, but they also work in the Park, as do most of the equine residents.

Numerous heavy horse breeds were developed to suit particular areas and different soil conditions. Mainland Europe had a great variety of breeds: the massive Ardennes, the Belgians, Jutlands, Bretons, Boulonnais and the French Percheron, possibly the most popular of all and widely exported. Britain had the majestic Shire Horse, the round, appealing Suffolk Punch and the hard-working Clydesdale.

RIGHT: *Mounted police play an important role in British regional police forces.*

After the Second World War, the outlook for the heavies seemed bleak, but they survived, perhaps largely because of the traditional loyalty of the great brewing companies, which made use of them to pull their splendid drays through the city streets to make urban deliveries. The heavies no longer exist in such numbers as previously but they enjoy greater popularity with the public than ever before, and this ensures their continued survival.

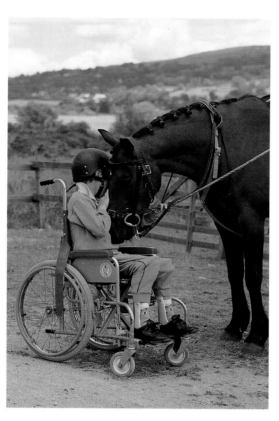

OPPOSITE: *The pomp and pageantry of H. M. the Queen's Household Cavalry, the Drums and Drum Horse of the Life Guards. By tradition the latter is a part-coloured horse.*
LEFT: *The Riding for the Disabled Association was formed in 1969 and there are now over 150 groups in Britain as well as many in other countries of the world. Every type of physical disability can be helped by regular riding under expert supervision.*
BELOW: *Riding holidays form a significant part of the modern holiday industry throughout the world. These riders are enjoying their horses on a quiet Tunisian beach in the sun.*

In forestry work throughout Europe, the horse plays an important role, hauling logs on steep hillsides, inaccessible to tractors.

One of the biggest areas providing work for the modern horse, however, is the holiday industry. In Scotland, for instance, where trekking was 'invented', this new holiday activity gave enormous encouragement to the breeding of the Highland pony. Riding holidays feature largely in America and throughout Europe. They are well organized, cover some of the most spectacular country in the world and attract thousands of people every year. You can even ride through India and China.

Finally, there is the most worthwhile use of horses and ponies in the rehabilitating therapy offered by the numerous branches of the Riding for the Disabled Association. Thousands of disabled children and adults benefit every week in every year from riding carefully selected ponies. Remarkable results can be achieved in terms of improved confidence, co-ordination, balance and mobility, and riding offers a new dimension to the lives of the disabled.

HORSE LANGUAGE

To understand why horses behave as they do and why, in human terms, they sometimes seem to act quite irrationally, we have to recognize that, despite thousands of years of domestication, the horse remains a herd animal governed by deeply ingrained instincts. These are supported by a set of highly developed senses, some of which, such as scent and touch, are used to communicate with other horses – and with humans, also, if they have learned the language.

Unlike the dog, which is carnivorous and aggressive, the horse is a grass-eating animal and non-aggressive, and that is the key to his character. It is true that horses have teeth with which they can bite, and legs that can deliver bone-breaking kicks, but these are not their primary purpose. The teeth are designed for eating a herbivorous diet, and the long legs allow the horse to escape from danger, or suspected danger, at high speed. With the horse it is always a matter of running first and asking no questions at all. The ability to take flight quickly is part of the horse's defence mechanism, along with its highly strung, nervous nature.

The position of the eyes gives all-round vision, even when grazing. The acute hearing, the heightened sense of smell, and a strange 'sixth sense' allow the horse to detect the presence of likely predators long before they are near enough to attack. For the domestic horse, such dangers as those encountered in the wild from predators like the mountain lion, or even the ultimate predator, man himself, no longer exist. The instinct, however, remains. Which is why a horse instinctively takes fright and shies at a scrap of paper rustling in the hedgerow. It is why unusual objects or noises make him unreasonably apprehensive – unreasonably, that is, from the human viewpoint.

In fact, despite the handicaps of a nature which fitted them for survival in the wild, and which is not entirely helpful or relevant in the domestic state, horses can display considerable intelligence and learn quickly.

RIGHT: *Play is also about establishing a dominant position within a group.*
BELOW: *Its gregarious, herd instinct is a strong motivation in the horse's behaviour.*

Horses and men

Like all animals, horses have the ability to communicate very well with members of their own species. For the most part, communication is made through a sophisticated body language supported by tactile signals and the sense of smell. The language is almost entirely dependent upon messages given and received by these means, but transmission can also be vocal, although whinnies, gentle whickering and the occasional angry scream comprise only the smallest part of the equine vocabulary.

It would, however, be unwise to assume that physical actions and the use of the natural senses constitute the sum total of the equine communication system. There is also a sixth sense, a heightened perception, which is apparent in the horse but rare in the human species. There are trainers of horses, and, indeed, of other animals, who are themselves sufficiently sensitive and positive to be able to respond to the horse's sensitivity and can, as it were, tune in to the horse's mental wavelength.

At least one authority talks of 'two disciplines involved in the human association with horses', the one concerned with physical signals, and the other, 'the over-lying discipline of the mind to which the physical actions must necessarily be surbservient'. Clearly, the communication between man and horse becomes more effective when the two are in balance.

If it is accepted that this sort of contact can exist between human and equine, it is reasonable to suppose that an even more effective communication will exist, on a similar basis, between two members of the same species.

BELOW: *A person can establish a relationship with the horse based on a mental empathy.*

The equine voice

Vocal communication is easily interpreted, but is of less importance than smell and touch, for example. A mare will whicker gently to reassure her foal, and most horses make the same noise in anticipation of feed-time or a titbit. Horses will whinny more loudly, the equivalent of a shout, if feed-times are delayed unduly. They also whinny in excitement, or if they have become separated from a close companion. Snorting indicates that the horse has seen or smelt something which interests it, or which it thinks may be a potential danger.

Squeals and grunts are usually associated with aggression. A mare who is not ready to mate will warn off an over-attentive suitor in this way, the message being reinforced by a threatening posture, bared teeth, laid-back ears and the hindlegs prepared to deliver a deterrent kick.

Conversely, the mare tells the stallion when she is ready to receive him by sending out several messages that are just as unmistakable. The physical message is made by adopting an opposite, mating, posture. She holds the tail to one side, and palpitates ('flashes') the vulva, indicating her availability quite clearly. Just as importantly, she attracts the stallion by producing a *pheromone*, a smell message produced by the skin glands.

BELOW LEFT: *The peculiar curling back of the lips ('flehmen') practised by stallions is often triggered by the presence of mares, but can also be associated with unusual smells.*

BELOW: *Instinctively, a foal gains confidence by being in close contact with its dam. Mares are very protective about their foals and become upset when separated from them.*

Scents and smells

The sense of smell plays a large part in equine communication. Stallions check the state of the mare's reproductive cycle by sniffing the vulva and the urine. This smelling may then be accompanied by licking the mare, involving the senses of taste and touch, and stimulating the mare sexually. When sexually excited, the stallion may also indulge in what is called *flehmen*, a peculiar curling back of the lips from the teeth. This action is not, however, always of sexual original, nor is it confined to stallions. Strong or unusual smells and/or tastes – garlic, lemon, or just the presence of worming powder in the food – will often produce the same response in both sexes.

Smell is much involved in the stallion's behaviour patterns; he scent-marks his 'territory', for instance, by urinating and depositing piles of droppings around its boundaries, even though the horse is not generally as 'territorial' as many animals. He will also urinate over the droppings of mares within his group, giving a warning to outsiders that the mares are under his protection. A stallion does this instinctively, and the behaviour persists even in domestic circumstances where there are no other competing stallions.

Foals recognize their dams by smell and it is probable that members of a group identify each other by a corporate scent. It is also likely that horses recognize their home surroundings in the same way, and it has been suggested that the sense of smell may be responsible for the homing instinct.

It is also well established that humans can communicate unconsciously by giving off odours indicating tension, fear, aggression and so on. The hyper-sensitive equine is well able to detect, by smell alone, a person who is nervous or frightened. Such a signal, sent out by the human, either causes the horse to become similarly nervous and apprehensive, or, if the animal is of a dominant nature, encourages aggression. Old time horsemen, such as the horse-tamers of the last century, would often smear their hands with some aromatic fluid to mask their own scent.

LEFT: *Mutual grooming is one way in which individuals establish a relationship.*

Taste and touch

The sense of taste is not perhaps so relevant to communication, other than being involved in the stallion's sexual advances, and, to a degree, being connected with the practice of mutual grooming, which plays a part in the establishment of relationships between individual horses.

Touch, however, is more important and more widely used. It is integral to sexual behaviour; it is evident in the mare and foal relationship, giving the foal a sense of security, and it is the principal element in mutual grooming. Furthermore, it is the main medium through which communication is possible between horse and human, for example through the signals made with a rider's hands and legs, which are called the aids. By squeezing with the legs, the rider requests a particular response from the horse, and once it has learnt the meaning of the signal, which is taught by a system combining repetition and reward, it will respond willingly – so long as the signal is given with unmistakable clarity and without any suggestion of force.

Grooming a horse is a way of establishing a reassuring relationship through the sense of touch. It links the human with the horse and contributes to a feeling of trust and security between the two.

The whiskers and the sensory nerves of the horse's muzzle are also involved with the sense of touch. By using them the horse is able to evaluate objects which it is unable to see; the contents of the manger, for instance. To trim the whiskers off for mere cosmetic effect, which is a common practice, is, therefore, to deprive the horse of part of the natural complement of senses.

It is noticeable that horses gain confidence by touching strange objects either with the nose or with a foot. Young horses, asked to cross a grid of trotting poles, will often peer down and touch the first one before completing the exercise. Before putting a saddle on a horse's back for the first time, it often helps if it has been placed in the manger, for instance, so that the horse is given the opportunity to touch it with its nose, thus effecting a reassuring introduction to the new piece of equipment.

ABOVE: *The act of grooming establishes a satisfying link between horse and human through the sense of touch.*

BELOW: *The rider communicates with the horse through physical signals, known as aids, made with the hands and the legs.*

Posture and behaviour

Visual communication through the adoption of particular postures can rarely be misunderstood. A horse that is relaxed and resting slackens the whole posture, possibly resting a hindleg. The head is dropped, the eyes partially closed, the ears droop and the lower lip may hang loose. The tense posture of an apprehensive horse is just as easily recognized. The head is raised, the eye enlarged and the ears stiffened; the whole outline, indeed, is tightened.

Stamping is an expression of impatience or irritation, not to be confused with striking out with the forefeet, which is an aggressive action. Sometimes, in order to gain more immediate attention, the stamping develops into the irritating habit of banging the stable door.

Presumably, too, the horse is attempting to put over some message – perhaps a cry for help – when it develops the habits of crib-biting, (gnawing the top of the stable door), wind-sucking, (swallowing air compulsively), or weaving (constantly swinging the head to and fro). Human beings interpret these equine efforts at communication as 'vices'.

Horses may express irritation at the attentions of a heavy-handed groom or a stiff-bristled brush by stamping, shaking the head and/or swishing the tail. Tail-swishing and head-shaking are penalized as resistances in dressage tests, which they sometimes are, although this can be an unjustified presumption by the judge.

Nothing, of course, so clearly indicates the horse's state of mind, and sometimes also its intentions, as the movement of the mobile and highly eloquent ears.

The hearing is exceptionally acute, the structure of the horse's head acting like a sound-box, while the ears are capable of almost complete rotation. Their range of movement, controlled by 13 pairs of muscles, adds expression to the face.

Ears pricked firmly forward indicate that the horse has seen something of interest, and at that moment it is unlikely to be distracted by signals from its rider. The ears are lowered and become flaccid when the horse is dozing. One stuck out sideways may mean nothing more than the presence of a buzzing fly.

Ears that flick back and forth when the horse is being ridden are reassuring to the rider, who knows that he has the horse's attention. Ears laid back, in conjunction with the white of the eye being displayed, indicate displeasure, temper or outright aggression. (Eyes and ears always operate in conjunction.)

Play-fighting is natural to young horses, and can include all the signs of aggression, but it is also a way in which an individual seeks to dominate a group and establish a pecking order. Although it may seem that the horses are at risk of sustaining an injury in these encounters, it is very rare for any harm to be done.

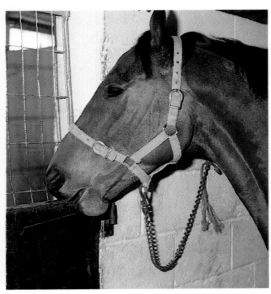

LEFT: *Bucking, as in this instance, and stamping are unmistakeable ways in which a horse will communicate its irritation and resentment to its rider.*
RIGHT: A *naturally relaxed group of horses enjoying the spring grass. There is no suggestion of tension in these animals.*
BELOW: *Conversely, this is a study in tension and stress. Crib-biting is one of the more familiar equine 'vices', but in fact, such irritating habits are probably only manifestations of the horse's insecurity.*

WHITE HORSES OF VIENNA

The Spanish Riding School of Vienna is the world's oldest academy of riding. For over 400 years it has been dedicated to the practice and preservation of the classical equestrian art in its purest form. Classical, school riding has its roots in the early schools of Naples, which in time gave way to the enlightened, rational systems exemplified by the later French Masters. The colossus of the equestrian art was François Robichon de la Guérinière (1688-1751), acknowledged as the 'Father of classical riding'. His work, expounded in the book *École de Cavalerie*, is as relevant today as in his own time, and his principles and precepts remain integral to the training carried out at the School.

The Spanish Riding School, so called because from its foundation it used Spanish horses, which up to the nineteenth century were the foremost breed in Europe, was established in about 1572 as an adjunct to the Hapsburg court, largely with the object of providing the nobility with an education in the equestrian arts. Originally it operated as the Spanish Riding Hall, in a simple wooden arena built adjacent to the Imperial Palace in Vienna.

The present School, known as the Winter Riding Hall, was founded as part of the Hofburg Palace in 1729 on the orders of the Emperor Charles VI. It was designed by Josef Emmanuel Fischer von Erlach and completed in 1735, when the vast Austro-Hungarian Empire was at the zenith of its power and influence. The magnificently galleried baroque central hall is 180 feet long, 59 feet wide and 56 feet high (55m×18m×17m) and at one end, above the imperial box, is the portrait of the School's founder, Charles VI. By tradition riders doff their bicorn hats in salute as they enter and leave the hall.

The famous Ladies Carousel of 1743, led by the Empress Maria Theresa, was the first great function to be held here and, for a century and a half, the Winter Riding Hall was used for all sorts of festivals, concerts and so on. The last carrousel took place in 1894, and thereafter the School was devoted exclusively to the 'training and demonstrating of horses and riders in the high art of horsemanship'.

RIGHT: *The* levade, *performed by a white Lipizzaner in the Winter Riding Hall, is the embodiment of the Spanish Riding School.*
BELOW: *Since 1920 the home of the Spanish School's Lipizzaner brood mares has been at the Piber Stud in Austria.*

'The noblest horse in the world'

The Spanish Riding School is so closely interlinked with the fortunes of the white Lipizzaner stallions that it is impossible to think of one without the other.

The Lipizzaners are descendants of Spanish horses, now termed Andalucian, that founded the stud at Lipizza (Lipica), from which they take their name, in 1580. In that year, the emissary of the Archduke Charles, youngest son of Emperor Ferdinand I and ruler of vast territories, procured and sent to Lipizza near Trieste (then a part of the Austro-Hungarian Empire), nine stallions and 24 mares from Iberia, an area that was in the possession of the Spanish Hapsburgs.

LEFT: *A good example of the Lipizzaner. The breed's equable temperament is well-suited to the disciplines of the* manège.
BELOW: *Foals are born black or brown, becoming white as they grow older. In accordance with genetic laws, there is the occasional bay.*

The object was to create a supply of superior horses, suitable for the ducal stables at Graz and the court stables at Vienna, that would be as impressive in harness as under saddle. Even today, Lipizzaners, outside those bred specifically for the Spanish School at Piber, (the home of the breed since 1920), are renowned as very fine carriage horses that do well in competitive driving events.

From the outset, deliberate attempts were made to breed white horses. From the earliest times, horses of this coat colour had been especially esteemed, and were considered the most suitable to the dignity of royalty – in this the House of Hapsburg was no exception. Nonetheless, other colours were common right up to the eighteenth century.

Pictures of brood mares at Lipizza show a whole range of coat colours. There are blacks, bays, duns and creams, as well as some spectacularly spotted coats. Early engravings of the period depict some striking spotted, piebald and skewbald horses executing the most advanced of the school movements, the electrifying 'leaps above the ground'.

Present day Lipizzaners of the Spanish School are, however, uniformly white, although the foals are born black and brown, becoming grey and then white as they grow older. In accordance with genetics, it is inevitable that there will be an occasional bay produced. These exceptions to the general rule are not used for breeding, but by tradition one is always kept at the School in Vienna.

It is not surprising that the Archduke Charles should have selected Spanish horses for his new stud. Indeed, for the purposes he required, there was no other horse that could have been considered. It was without doubt the best horse in Europe, the most valuable and the one most suited, both physically and in temperament, to the demanding disciplines of the *manège*. It was, wrote William Cavendish, Duke of Newcastle and the sole English Master of the equestrian art, 'the noblest horse in the world . . . and fittest of all for a King in the day of Triumph.' For a period of some 300 years, no reigning monarch or victorious commander would have dreamt of being painted or sculpted on anything other than a proudly prancing Spanish horse.

The Lipizza stud

The choice of Lipizza as a site for the stud is not so immediately understandable, but there were sound reasons for choosing this small village in the harsh, inhospitable Karst country at the upper end of the Adriatic. Today it is in the north-west of modern Yugoslavia, and horses are still bred there. The terrain is predominantly limestone, and limestone is an essential factor in the rearing of young stock, for it produces good, hard bone and excellent feet. Additionally, as the Romans had discovered centuries before, this area of sparse vegetation dominated by stony outcrops was an ideal breeding ground for hardy stock that developed a strong constitution and was inherently sound. The horses matured slowly, but in consequence enjoyed a remarkable longevity, a notable characteristic of the modern Lipizzaner. Many of the stallions at Vienna are performing the difficult advanced exercises at well over 20 years of age and it is not unusual for them to live beyond 30. In fact, the Lipizzaner does not thrive in an easier, more lush environment.

During the turbulent history of the breed, when the successive wars which swept through Europe compelled the subsequent evacuation of the horses, it was found that the essential character of the Lipizzaner could only be retained in a similar habitat to that of the rocky Karst. Lipizza was twice evacuated during the French wars, and in 1915 the horses were moved to the studs at Laxenburg and Kladrub, before finally being settled at Piber in Austria in 1920. Except for an enforced sojourn at Hostau during the Second World War, the School horses have been bred there ever since. When the stud was at Laxenburg, where the soil conditions did not suit the horses, many were lost and the fertility and birth rates dropped dramatically.

LEFT: *Numbers of Lipizzaners are still raised at their traditional home at Lipizza in the Yugoslavian Karst country. The rocky terrain is predominantly limestone and the horses develop good, hard bone and excellent feet. A riding school devoted to the classical art is also maintained at Lipizza and operates on the same principles as the Spanish School.*

The Lipizzaner bloodlines

Spanish horses continued to be bought for the Stud up to the eighteenth century, when their popularity made it difficult to obtain the type required. The problem was overcome by outcrosses to Italian stock, the closely related Neapolitans from Polesina and Naples itself, and by horses obtained from Germany and the Royal Danish Stud at Frederiksborg. All these horses, however, were of pure Spanish descent, or almost so. The exception was a white Arabian stallion, Siglavy, and his influence on the Lipizzaner bloodlines was profound.

Siglavy joined the stud in 1816, as a six-year-old, at a time when the Thoroughbred horse was firmly established and was being used extensively to upgrade stock throughout Europe. Efforts were made to introduce Thoroughbred blood to the compact, stocky Lipizzaners, but they were never successful and were soon abandoned.

From this situation, six principal stallion lines were established to which all modern Lipizzaners at the Spanish Riding School can be traced. Their direct descendants can be seen performing the majestic patterns of the School quadrille in the Winter Riding Hall to this day.

The foundation stallions, their memory perpetuated by the practice of using their names as a prefix to those of their progeny, are these:

PLUTO: white, born in 1765 of pure Spanish descent and obtained from the Royal Danish Stud. (The Danish Stud developed its own breed, the Frederiksborg).
CONVERSANO: a black Neapolitan horse, born in 1767.
FAVORY: a dun horse from the Bohemian Kladrub Stud, born in 1779. (The Kladrub Stud was founded in 1572 by Maximilian II to provide coach horses for the Imperial carriages. Subsequently it was much influenced by the Spanish stock of Lipizza).

TOP RIGHT: A Lipizzaner stallion in front of one of the old and original buildings at Lipizza, where the Archduke Charles founded his court stud of Spanish horses in 1580.
RIGHT: The mares at Lipizza differ a little from those kept at Piber and, indeed, elsewhere in Europe. They are, nonetheless, unmistakable representatives of this famous breed.

SIGLAVY: the pure-bred white Arabian, born in 1810.
MAESTOSO: a white horse, born in 1819 at the most important of the great Hungarian studs, Mezöhegyes. He was by a Neapolitan stallion out of a Spanish dam.

Of the original mare lines, 14 are still preserved at Piber.

The Lipizzaner of carriage type can be as large as 16.1 hands high, but the Piber-bred School horses are not much more than an inch or two over 15 hands. The type produced conforms virtually to the baroque pattern, which has not changed much in 300 years. It is a compact horse of the type that the English would describe as being 'stuffy'. It has notably strong limbs and is very powerful in the quarters and in the naturally crested neck. Sometimes it retains the ram nose of the old Spanish breed, but an Eastern influence, through Siglavy, is also apparent. It is by no means built to gallop, and the action is frequently elevated, but it is agile and athletic. Moreover, it has an ideal temperament and is intelligent. The Lipizzaner learns quickly and performs happily within the strict school disciplines without loss of spirit.

The Spanish School this century

The Spanish Riding School, alone among the numerous court schools of Europe, survived the disintegration of the ramshackle Austro-Hungarian Empire in 1918. Its jealously preserved traditions ensured that the School was integral to Viennese culture, and the new Republic of Austria continued to maintain it as a cultural institution which was open to the public during training sessions and for regular performances.

Remarkably, the School survived the chaos of the Second World War, and did so largely through the good offices of an American, General George Patton, himself a cavalryman. In 1945, at the end of hostilities, the Lipizzaner horses from Piber, as well as those from the state studs of neighbouring countries, were at the remount depot at Hostau and in danger of falling into the hands of the advancing Russians. Patton, following a plea from the School's Director, Colonel Alois Podhajsky, placed the old School under his personal protection, and Task Force Reed, under Colonel Charles Reed, brought the horses back to Piber on 28 April 1945.

ABOVE: A *Lipizzaner of the School at Lipizza in Yugoslavia, the breed's traditional home. Displays are given daily at the School.*

BELOW: A bereiter *of the Spanish School demonstrating the paces and movements of a Lipizzaner stallion in the long reins.*

Training the stallions

Each year, in October, eight to ten young stallions, aged three and a half years, are brought from Piber to the Stallburg, the building which has housed the white horses of the School since 1565. The first eight to ten weeks of their training is spent familiarizing the young horses with their new surroundings and getting them used to the concept of regular work. That work begins with exercises on the lunge, and prepares the horse for carrying a rider's weight, backing (mounting by the rider) being carried out at the end of the period.

The rest of the first year is devoted to straightforward basic riding, largely in straight lines or gentle curves, during which time the young horse gradually acquires a natural balance under his rider.

In the second year of training, referred to as the 'lower or campaign school', the progressive gymnastic exercises lead to increased collection, i.e. the lowering of the croup; increased engagement of the hindlegs, shortening the base; raising of the forehand and improved carriage of head and neck: in fact the compression of the horse's powers. At the end of this stage, the horse is ready to be taught the advanced High School movements of *piaffe*, *passage* etc. – the 'airs on the ground' – and will be assessed for his aptitude for the most difficult movements, the School leaps, or 'airs above the ground'. The former are included in the Grand Prix dressage test, but the leaps do not form part of competitive dressage.

The third and fourth years of training belong to the *Haute École* or High School. The horse becomes confirmed in the flying change of leg at the canter (the leading leg being changed in the air, giving the impression that the horse is dancing to the music which always accompanies the School performances). He is taught to execute the beautiful pirouette movement with fluency, and learns the very difficult *piaffe* and *passage* (Spanischer Tritt). The latter is an elevated, collected trot, of slow, majestic cadence, the horse moving straight, without any lateral swinging of the quarters. *Piaffe* is *passage* executed virtually on the spot, the pace being marked by its cadence and regularity.

ABOVE: *A gala performance in the Winter Riding Hall, held under the portrait of the School's founder, the Emperor Charles VI.*

BELOW: *The exercises on the lunge form the basis of the young stallion's education and prepare him to carry the rider's weight.*

The airs above the ground

Especially talented horses are then taught the 'airs above the ground', which are first practised in-hand. Only when the horse is well able to perform the leaps without weight on his back is he asked to execute them under a rider.

The leaps are regarded as the highest point in the classical art, and the ultimate manifestation of complete collection. They derive from the movements taught to the war-horse of the mounted knight and used to discourage the close proximity of foot soldiers intent on unhorsing the rider. Whether, in fact, the leaps performed at Vienna bear much resemblance to the deterrent kicks and jumps made in an emergency on the medieval fields of battle is a matter for debate. They should, perhaps, be regarded as supreme refinements of a medieval ideal which had little basis in reality.

In seventeenth-century Europe there were no less than seven classical leaps. Today, only the three primary leaps are performed, and the seventeenth-century variations, amounting often to less than complete movements, are excluded.

The three are *levade*, *courbette* and the soaring *capriole* (the 'leap of the goat', from the Italian word *capra* meaning goat).

In *levade*, the forehand is lifted on deeply bent hindlegs, the hocks being lowered to some 8-10in (20-25cm) above the ground, while the forelegs are bent. The position is held for a short length of time.

Levade is the basis for *courbette*, the horse bounding forward on the hindlegs while maintaining the bent foreleg position. The ultimate extension of both movements is when the horse leaps from all four legs simultaneously in the *capriole*, striking out with the hindlegs whilst the body is virtually suspended in mid-air.

TOP LEFT: *The soaring leap of the* capriole, *the ultimate air above the ground, performed in-hand at Vienna.*

LEFT: *The* levade, *which, like all the airs above the ground, is performed without stirrups, is the basis for the two more extravagant leaps, the* courbette *and the* capriole. *The movements are said to derive from those taught to the war horses of the medieval knights.*

The Spanish School in performance

Only stallions are used at the school, and for the twice-weekly performances they wear black bridles with gold buckles and the traditional white buckskin saddle, the *selle royale*. The riders wear the equally traditional dark brown tailcoats, cocked hats, buckskin breeches and high black boots. The whips they carry are long, unembellished birch switches; they are practical but also serve as a symbol of the rider's humility – a pleasing thought.

The riders are all Austrian citizens, and it takes four to six years for them to be taught to ride a fully trained horse and another two to four years before they are capable of training a horse to this standard.

The elegant Quadrilles, the *pas de deux* and other parts of the School programme are accompanied by the music of Bizet, Chopin, Mozart and Boccherini, and when the dancing white horses and their uncannily still riders enter under the great chandeliers, the audience witnesses the rare beauty of 'the art of riding cultivated in its purest form and brought to perfection'.

RIGHT: *The brilliant* pas de deux *is ridden to the music of Bizet and Chopin under the Winter Riding Hall's priceless chandeliers.*
BELOW: *At halt, complete immobility of horse and rider is required.*

HORSES IN HARNESS

The wheel, the prime factor in the use of horses in harness, made its appearance at a very early date. Solid wheels, like those used in the bullock carts of the East to this day, were probably being made before the time when the horse was first domesticated. Possibly they were developed from rollers placed under a sledge to make its movement easier. Such rollers, and evidence of solid wheels, were found in the excavation of Sumerian graves in the area of the Tigris-Euphrates valley, and they have been dated at about 3500 BC. More sophisticated wheels, with spokes, were developed about 1,000 years after that date, and war-chariots, the forerunners of the elegant-wheeled vehicles of the eighteenth and nineteenth centuries, were commonplace throughout the Middle East by that time and were employed in great numbers in the battles of antiquity.

The Chinese, a people who, although their culture was not so dependent on horses, made the greatest contribution of all to the concept of the driven horse, had chariots and two-wheeled pleasure and travelling vehicles of surprisingly modern design as much as 3,300 years ago.

Under the Ch'in dynasty, during which the Great Wall of China was completed to an unbroken length of 1,400 miles (2,253km), there was a standardization of the writing system, of weights and measures, and, importantly in this context, of axle widths, allowing roadways to be used more effectively. There were three road categories; one for narrow-gauge vehicles, another for broad-gauge and a third, like a dual-carriageway, which was wide enough for wagons to pass each other.

Nor did the Chinese neglect the methods by which horses could be harnessed to vehicles or, indeed, the breeding of suitable horses. In the seventh century they established breeding studs, which produced three-quarters of a million horses for specific purposes, mostly peaceful.

The Chinese were the inventors of shafts for single-horse vehicles, the first people to drive horses in tandem (one behind the other), and by 250 BC had produced the breast harness. After that came the breeching strap, which passes round the quarters allowing the horse's weight to slow the vehicle, and finally the horse collar, claimed as one of the world's greatest inventions, for it allowed the most efficient use of tractive force.

RIGHT: *Traditional Dutch turnout of a pair of Friesians to a Friesian cart.*
BELOW: *A team tackles a water obstacle with confidence on a cross-country driving course.*

Harnessed for work

For a long time, Europe was far behind the civilizations of China and the Middle East. It was not until the eighth century that harness and horseshoes were sufficiently developed for horses to carry out agricultural work, and at that time the animals were not big enough to undertake more than a limited range of tasks. It was to be another 200 years before the predecessors of today's heavy horse breeds evolved, and many centuries were to pass before the elegant and superbly finished driving vehicles, with which we are familiar today, would be perfected.

Much of the credit for the design of coaches and carriages in the eighteenth and nineteenth centuries is due to the Hungarians, who to this day figure most prominently in driving sports. It was their predecessors, the Huns, who first came to Europe with wheeled transport. Attila had a wagon-laager, or encampment, at the battle of the Catalaunian fields, and Hungarians were operating wagon-train systems when the rest of Europe was dependent upon pack transport. Their wagons and equipment provided the pattern for the rest of Europe, and the road coach that was to be the glory of the English highways was first produced in prototype during the late fifteenth century, long before there was anything approaching a smooth roadway in Britain.

The first coaches were made in the Komorne area of Hungary, at the village of Kocs, a place famous for its wainwrights. The coach (*kocsi*) takes its name from the village. The front wheels of the Hungarian vehicle were smaller than the rear ones, which allowed the fore-carriage to turn on a very wide lock. (The same arrangement was a feature of a wagon buried with the Sumerian King Abargi in about 3000 BC!)

Such a vehicle had the advantage of a lower centre of gravity, allowing it to be driven faster, and it was, moreover, much lighter than any contemporary vehicle. Another Hungarian innovation was to support the light body of the coach on leather slings like a hammock. Then came the final development, the multi-leaved elliptical spring, which not only increased the comfort of the vehicle, but also greatly improved its performance and safety.

Thereafter, particularly in England, improved axle-box patterns were introduced, leading to fewer broken axles and lost wheels, which had previously caused many accidents, and significant advances were also made in the design and construction of harness. Walsall, in England, became the centre of the world's leather goods and harness fittings trade, and remained so for 200 years. Harness became much lighter with the use of better quality leather and improvements in the design of fittings and buckles.

ABOVE LEFT: A *sleigh ride on the snow is an attraction of the Swiss resort of St Moritz.*
LEFT: *Going to a horse-show in appropriate style in Hungary, the land of horses and horsemen and home of the coach.*
RIGHT: *HRH Prince Michael competing in the dressage phase at the Windsor Driving Championships.*

Competitive driving

The coaching era, which was made possible in England by a road system unequalled elsewhere in Europe together with the availability of the best horses, did not, for all the legend and romance of the open road, last beyond the middle of the nineteenth century. It marked, indeed, the culmination of a great driving tradition, and at the same time it became the inspiration for 'private driving'. In England the Four-in-Hand Club was formed in 1856, and in 1871 the prestigious Coaching Club. They still survive today, when the popularity of driving seems greater than ever.

There were, indeed, many earlier clubs formed in the previous century, when driving was a fashionable pastime for young sporting bloods and was sponsored enthusiastically by the Prince of Wales, later George IV. Wealthy young bucks imitated the crack coachmen of the day, copying their form of dress and speech, and even having their teeth filed, the better to be able to whistle through them.

The Prince Regent was an accomplished whip, frequently driving himself, and on at least one occasion he drove a random (three horses harnessed in front of each other, tandem fashion) from London to the Pavilion at Brighton. This was an unusual

feat, and one demanding great skill, but it paled in comparison with some of the wagers and matches in which the sporting set of the eighteenth century delighted.

There are hundreds of examples of remarkable races and exploits, many of them involving specially built vehicles. In the last years of the sixteenth century Captain John Gibb won £500 – then a vast sum – by driving a four-in-hand up and down the steepest part of the Devil's Ditch on Newmarket Heath. He used a jointed connecting rod between the front and rear wheels of his light chaise so that the vehicle could cope with the undulations of the ground, and he dispensed with the pole between the two wheel horses, harnessing them loosely. (A pair of horses are usually hitched one each side of a central pole).

LEFT: A *splendid team of greys enter the water from a downhill approach during the driving trials cross-country phase.*
BELOW: *This charming American Shetland, harnessed to a light, four-wheeled show buggy, displays an excellent harness action.*

Another match on Newmarket Heath, in the next century, was between the Earls of March and Eglintowne, and Messrs Sproule and Taafe, for a wager of £1,000. They matched teams of four Thoroughbred horses, postillion driven and drawing the lightest possible four-wheeled carriage, carrying one passenger, over 19 miles (30km). The journey was completed by the noble Earls in 53 minutes 27 seconds, with the horses running away for the first four miles (six kilometres).

In England, individual enthusiasts, including the eighth Duke of Beaufort, and the American, Alfred Vanderbilt, ran privately owned coaches over the old routes up to the time of the First World War, and even after that a number of coaches continued to run until 1939 and the outbreak of the Second World War.

Coaching meets, as well as private driving meets for pairs and single carriages, are still held regularly, and driving classes, as well as the exciting timed scurry competitions around a course of obstacles, are a feature at most horse shows.

Post-war driving soon took on a competitive image in both Europe and America. On the continental mainland, the sport of cross-country driving was well established and standards were very high. That it became an internationally recognized sport was due to another British Prince, HRH the Duke of Edinburgh. He became interested when he watched the competitions at Aachen in 1968, as President of the International Equestrian Federation (F.E.I.), and he instigated the first international event in 1970.

Horse driving trials, now a major equestrian discipline for singles, pairs and teams, are based on the ridden three-day-event format, with an extra turnout phase called Presentation. After this there is a dressage test, and then Competition B, the Marathon, the equivalent of the ridden speed and endurance phase. The Marathon course includes all sorts of hazards and obstacles, and can be as long as 17 miles (27km). The final phase is obstacle driving, which, like showjumping in Horse Trials, tests the continued fitness of the horses.

Team driving horses and Trotters

A wide variety of horses and ponies can be used for driving. For scurry competitions there is little to beat quick, handy ponies such as the Welsh, but Shetlands and part-breds of all sorts can hold their own. Prince Philip has recently driven a team of Fell ponies, having previously competed with teams of powerful Cleveland Bay crosses. Welsh Cobs, or Cob crosses, are ideal driving horses, too. They are not too long in the body, which helps when turning a team of four through a complex obstacle, they are fast enough and also very courageous and enduring.

BELOW: *A crack Hungarian driving team waste no time on a section of the marathon drive. These horses are particularly well matched.*

The Hungarians often use the carriage-type Lipizzaner, bigger and with more scope than those bred at Piber for the Spanish School, and their ornate harness is light and ideally suited to their dashing style of driving. Instead of curb bits, the horses wear double-ring snaffles and they go in a breast harness rather than in the conventional driving collar.

The Germans have a number of Warmbloods on which to call; horses such as the powerful Oldenburg, Holstein and Hanoverian crosses, while a number of competitors make use of the impressive, upstanding Gelderlanders of the Netherlands – an exemplary pattern of carriage horse.

Although driving is an increasingly popular sport and pastime in the western world, it cannot approach the enormous following enjoyed by harness racing, which extends into New Zealand and Australia.

Both these countries have a strong harness racing, or trotting, tradition.

In America it is the second most popular sport after Thoroughbred racing, attracting gates that, in total, exceed 30 million, and are far in excess of those attracted by American football, for instance.

In Italy, more trotting horses are bred than Thoroughbreds, and in France the sport is as popular as flat-racing and has been firmly established since the early nineteenth century. Indeed, it has resulted in the development of an important breed, the tough French Trotter, which evolved as a result of crossing strong, but rather coarse, Norman mares with English Thoroughbreds and half-breds, as well as with the incomparable Norfolk Roadster. There are more than 30 raceways in France, headed by the Hippodrome de Vincennes where the 1.2 mile (2km) track is recognized as the supreme test for a harness trotter.

In other European countries and Scandinavia, harness racing is the principal equestrian sport, as it is in Russia, a country that has also developed its own breed from the purpose-bred Orlov Trotter.

Only in Britain, the country that did more than any other to establish the trotting breeds through its Thoroughbreds and Norfolk Roadsters, or Trotters, has the sport never captured the public imagination. (The Roadsters have long since ceased to exist.) It is practised, in a minor way, at raceways in the Midlands, North Wales and Lancashire, and at grass tracks elsewhere, but has never become a major sport.

The leading harness racing nation is without doubt America, which has had the greatest influence on the sport throughout the world, largely because of the American Standardbred, the world's foremost harness-racer. Today there are over 70 major raceways in the USA, all constructed to the same standard design. They are oval in shape, left-handed, and equipped with mobile starting gates, all-weather surfaces and floodlighting, evening races being the rule rather than the exception. Most tracks stage at least 50 meetings a year, and some have as many as 200.

While the British gentry of the eighteenth century were preoccupied with the development of the Thoroughbred, and as a result neglected the country's great trotting tradition, American colonists were laying the foundations of the sport and creating their own breed of trotting horse, founded on an imported Thoroughbred, Messenger. This horse, which arrived in America in 1788 after having raced successfully on the flat in England, was by Mambrino, and he had crosses to all three of the Arabian foundation sires. Messenger never raced in harness, but his sire did, and his owner, Lord Grosvenor, once offered to match him for 1,000 sovereigns to trot 14 miles (22km) to the hour. Mambrino was a grandson of Sampson, by Blaze, of a line of patriarchal trotters. There was, of course, much good Roadster blood in the early evolution of the Thoroughbred.

Messenger spent 20 years at stud in Pennsylvania, New York and New Jersey, dying at the age of 28 on Long Island in 1808. During that time he was bred to all sorts of mares, including Morgans and the Canadian and Narragansett Pacers. The last two no longer exist, but they contained much of the old Spanish jennet's 'ambling' or pacing blood, and they introduced the lateral pacing gait, the legs moving in lateral pairs rather than in diagonals as in the conventional trot.

BELOW: *Ponies may not be as fast as horses but a team takes up less room when negotiating obstacles and they are hardier.*

In America, pacers, which are never raced against conventional trotters, now outnumber the latter by four to one. In Europe conventional trotters are more numerous, but only just.

The slightly faster pacer is preferred in the States, where heavy betting is a feature of the sport, because their action, assisted by hobbles, is less likely to break than that of a trotting horse. If a horse breaks pace, it is penalized by having to move to the outside and loses ground.

The foundation sire of the Standardbred was Messenger's closely inbred descendant, Hambletonian 10, foaled in 1849. He, too, never raced in harness, but he sired no less than 1,335 offspring between 1851 and 1875. Nearly all Standardbreds now registered in the Stud Books descend from him, through four principal bloodlines represented by his most notable sons.

The term Standardbred was first used in 1879, and derives from the practice of establishing a speed standard as a requirement for entry into the Register (the *Trotting Register* was first published by John H. Wallace in 1871). The original standard was a mile (1.5km) in three minutes, later set at 2.30 minutes for trotters and 2.25 minutes for pacers.

The first sub-2 minute mile was paced by Star Pointer in 1897, and from then on speeds became continually faster, particularly after the introduction, in 1892, of the light bike-wheel sulky with pneumatic tyres.

In 1938 the mighty Greyhound paced the mile in 1.55.25 minutes, a record that stood for 31 years. The all-time record for the mile, of 1.52.1 minutes, was set in 1987 by the American pacer Mack Lobell, although Niatross time-trialed a remarkable 1.49.5 minutes at Lexington's Red Mile in 1980.

LEFT: *This Standardbred at Lexington's Red Mile raceway wears a shadow roll noseband and full pacing hobbles.*
RIGHT: *A Standardbred trotting conventionally to a light exercise sulky. The majority of harness racers are pacing horses, which, with the assistance of hobbles, are less likely to break the gait than are trotting horses. Horses breaking the gait must pull over to the outside and lose ground in consequence.*
BELOW: *Driving a harness racer over a mile in under two minutes is a sport demanding exceptional skills of the drivers.*

THE CIRCUS HORSE

In the classical civilizations of both Greece and Rome, the circus played a large part. It is true that the Roman circus, deliberately staged to distract an often riotous and potentially rebellious populace, included horrific spectacles of cruelty and death, as well as chariot races that resembled a battlefield, but it also included equestrian 'acts', which displayed the performers' great skill and artistry.

Acrobatics of all sorts were performed on horseback, and trick riding was popular. 'Roman riding', for instance, in which the artist gallops two horses round the arena with one foot on the back of each, is an act that has been performed in circuses all over the world for 2,000 years or more, if sometimes under different titles – the 'Hungarian Gallop' for instance.

After the fall of the Roman Empire, the Byzantine circus continued the tradition, and its displays were a powerful early influence on the growth of classical riding. Both Grisone, the first classical master of the sixteenth century School of Naples, and his most famous pupil, Giovanni Baptista Pignatelli, studied and learnt from the methods of the Byzantines. A riding academy, a *circus*, was established in Constantinople in 536, and there is evidence to show that it was very familar with the parade pace called *tripudium*, which would be recognized today as *piaffe*, as well as some recognizable 'airs above the ground' (see page 80).

In fact, the circus, in which for centuries the horse acts were central, has a strong connection with advanced equitation. In its heyday in nineteenth-century France, the circus was an entertainment of often grand proportions, which attracted the élite of society. François Baucher, the intuitive genius of the French school, exhibited his art and his horses in the *Cirque d'Été* in Paris, as did James Fillis, who became Chief Instructor at the Cavalry School in Leningrad. The crowds thronged to see horsemen, and horsewomen, of this calibre demonstrating the airs of *Haute École*, but the acknowledged creator of the modern circus was an Englishman, Philip Astley (1742-1814).

RIGHT: *The famous Roman Ride has been performed in circuses for over 2,000 years.*
BELOW: *Jasmin Smart's brilliant display of Liberty horses. All are pure-bred Arabians.*

The history of the circus

Philip Astley had been a Sergeant-Major in Elliot's 15th Light Horse, and had then served in the forces of the King of Prussia. At the age of 24, having served gallantly in the Seven Years War, he left the service, with the gift of a white horse he called Gibraltar. Astley was a good horseman, light and athletic, and had excelled at the mounted games which even then were part of military training.

In civilian life, having married into a circus family, he first earned his living giving demonstrations of trick riding and acrobatics with Gibraltar, but was soon able to open his first circus, Astley's Amphitheatre, in a field near the present site of London's Waterloo Station.

The regular riding *manège* had always been rectangular, but in 1769 Astley built a circular track fenced in with a covered stand, and ten years later added a roof to it, at the same time changing the name to the more grandiloquent The Astley Royal Amphitheatre of Arts.

Astley had learnt, by practice, that when galloping on a small circle it was possible to stand more easily on a horse's back, without losing balance, because of the resultant centrifugal force. His riding circle was 42 feet (13m) in diameter, and the circus ring has been so ever since, although some authorities credit Laurent and Henri Franconi, sons of a later partner of Astley, with the actual standardization in size of the ring. The Franconis were members of a circus dynasty who developed the great French circus tradition and were responsible for many of the most famous equestrian acts and stunts.

The size of Astley's arena may, it has been suggested, have been chosen out of a gypsy tradition which accords particular importance to certain magic figures, but it is far more likely that it was the horse, and the act, that determined the size. A standardized ring allowed an animal to appear in any one of the 19 circuses subsequently established by Astley, without having to adapt the smooth gait and rhythm it had acquired to rings of different sizes. The rhythm, the smoothness of the movement, and the constant angle at which the horse inclines towards the centre, are

ABOVE: *Many popular equestrian circus acts have their origin in the trick-riding of the* czikos, *the Hungarian cowboy.*

RIGHT: *The Hungarians are natural horsemen and very skilful in teaching horses to perform all sorts of movements.*

absolutely critical to the performance of bareback stunts.

Astley, who achieved an international reputation, was not only a skilful performer, but also a consummate showman, presenting his acts with flair and bravura. To his horse acts he added others: clowns, acrobats, jugglers, tightrope artists, a dog trainer and so on.

The name 'circus' does not seem to have been used by Astley. It is from the Latin for ring, and first appeared in 1782 when Charles Hughes, a former rider with Astley, opened his own Royal Circus on the south bank of the Thames, not far away from Astley's Amphitheatre.

Astley died without issue in 1814, but his partner, the Venetian Antonio Franconi, continued to expand the concept of circus entertainment with his Olympic Circus in Paris and *Le Cirque d'Hiver* (the Winter Circus), on the Boulevard des Filles du Calvaire, in the same city. His circuses often performed before huge crowds in vast marquees, and he developed a wide variety of animal acts, including enormous numbers of ponies and horses.

Franconi, an Italian gentleman by birth, who was forced to leave his own country after killing a rival in a duel, began his circus career in Rouen, where, in 1786, he performed his famous 'ribbon leap', somersaulting from the backs of two galloping horses over ribbons held outstretched, and landing on his feet on the horses' backs on the other side. He is also credited with the Royal, or St Petersburg, Pass, in which the rider stood balanced on two horses and controlled, using extra long reins, six or eight others performing wheels and circles around him.

In Paris, particularly, but also in St Petersburg and Moscow, the circus was firmly established in the nineteenth century as a smart entertainment for fashionable society, on a par with the opera and the ballet. Numerous painters were attracted by the colour, the magic of the lights, and the glittering sequins, and captured some of the wonder of the circus on their canvases. Artists of the calibre of Degas and Toulouse-Lautrec, and more recently Laura Knight, and even Picasso, came under the spell of the sawdust ring.

The great circus riders

Initially the circus equestrian acts had been concerned mainly with exhibitions of *Haute École*, presented by gifted civilian horsemen and women who used the ring as a showcase, and who, like all other circus performers, had something of the showman in their makeup. Fillis, for instance, used the circus as a medium for displaying his virtuosity and his absolute control of the horse. Some of the movements he rode were not exactly classical, but their execution was assessed and applauded by appreciative and expert audiences. He could produce movements like the *lancade*, a half-rear executed with either foreleg extended, and he rode, in perfect balance, the canter to the rear on three legs!

There were, too, the great trick riders, such as the Englishman Andrew Ducrow, who appeared in vast horse spectacles, like equestrian pantomimes, initially called 'military glories'. Later, Buffalo Bill Cody was to extend the idea to his Wild West shows. Gradually, however, the importance of serious equestrian display gave way to more frivolous turns, although many of the great circus owners continued to present horse acts which, for sheer horsemanship, could never be surpassed. The Renz family, and in particular the great equestrienne Thérèse Renz, who was performing her *Haute École* act at the age of 80 on Thoroughbred horses she trained herself, were riders in the classical tradition, and the Schumanns are as gifted as any horse trainers in the world.

The glamorous equestrienne was always the star of the circus. One of the first was Carolina Loyo, who was trained by François Baucher, and presented acts with him. She was really a bareback ballerina, specializing in her own versions of the ribbon and hoop leaps. Paulina Schumann was famous for her performances with the Arab stallion Suliman, the finale of their act being to exit the ring with Suliman walking on his hind legs. Lady riders are also regularly featured in the highly professional displays given by the Cossacks

LEFT: *The glamorous Carol Svensson's acrobatic* pas de deux, *which delighted audiences at London's Olympia in the eighties.*

of the enormous Moscow State Circus, which is as great a cultural institution in the USSR as the Bolshoi. The Iriston Riders, a breakneck Cossack group which regularly performs outside Russia, was led, until recently, by the woman *Haute École* star, Dzerassa Touganova.

There have been some lady *Haute École* riders who combined their equestrian art with that of the striptease. Lilo, of the Paris Médrano Circus, completed her act on her white Lipizzaner clad in no more than a very brief gold-sequinned bikini. Monique Montez, who doubled as a nightclub artiste, was another equestrian stripper, whilst Adah Menken was billed as performing her act entirely without clothes. In fact, she wore flesh-coloured tights.

A present day circus superstar is Mary Chipperfield of the Chipperfield circus family. She has shown groups of Lipizzaner and Arab Liberty horses, rides *Haute École* routines, and presents all sorts of novelty acts. In addition, she is just as much at home working with tigers as with horses.

RIGHT: *Michael Austin of the Austin Bros. Circus in a Wild West act that employed a heavy, rosin-back horse.*
BELOW: *A comic circus act called Little and Large. Large, in fact, was a Grand Prix dressage horse and the handlers of both horses are skilled trainers and dressage riders.*

The performing horses

Circus horses fall into three main groupings: the *Haute École* horse, usually Thoroughbred but sometimes Arab or Lipizzaner; Liberty horses, which are often Arabs and are shorter than the Thoroughbred, which because of his length, takes up more room in the ring; and finally the rosin-back or vaulting horse. The rosin-back may be a draught horse, or at least a heavily built animal. Circuses, of course, favour the spectacular spotted horses, such as the old sort of Knabstrup, and sometimes they use the coal-black Friesians. Whatever the horse, it must have a wide back and an imperturbable temperament, as well as being able to canter rhythmically. Shetlands and Welsh Ponies are always popular and often take part in mixed animal acts.

Circus horses, always cared for to the highest standards, are only lightly worked, being exercised for half an hour or so a day, and then performing in the ring for two ten-minute sessions. Most of them, as a result, live to a ripe old age.

RIGHT: *Arabian Liberty horses, which are shorter than Thoroughbreds, are often used in circuses. These talented ones not only balanced on their hindlegs to command but could also walk round the ring and make their exit on two legs.*
FAR RIGHT: *The most difficult animal acts are those that use a number of different animals. This donkey and monkey partnership combined very successfully with elephants and clowns.*
BELOW: *There is more than a breath of the circus about this arresting costume display given by John Lassetter, one of Britain's leading dressage trainers, and two of his pupils on Lassetter's highly schooled Lipizzaner stallions.*

EQUINE EXOTICS

For some 10,000 years the horse was extinct on the American continent, only being re-introduced by the Spanish *conquistadores* of the sixteenth century. Christopher Columbus had arrived at Hispaniola, now Haiti, in 1490, bringing with him 30 horses from the Old World. In 1506, when Columbus died, the Spanish had established breeding centres in the West Indies. Thirteen years later, Hernan Cortes (1485-1547) landed in Mexico and, with a force of 1,600 Spaniards and 16 horses, conquered the Aztec nation. In 1532 another Spanish adventurer, Francisco Pizarro, the brutal conqueror of the Inca nation, is credited with having taken the first horses to South America.

Cortes' horses were documented in considerable detail. There were 11 stallions, two of which were spotted or particoloured, and 11 mares. All came from the Cordoba strain, and they carried not only the colour genes which were once a feature of the Spanish horses, but also much of the lateral pacing or ambling movement for which the small Spanish horses called jennets had been famous throughout the Old World since the Middle Ages.

In the space of a mere 400 years from that momentous conquest, America became the most powerful nation on earth, and could boast a horse population of more than twenty-five million, which at one time represented a ratio of one horse to every three people.

Typically, the American genius for innovative, uninhibited adaptation resulted in the evolution of breeds and types that were remarkable in their variety, and were sometimes unique.

No country has such a range of coat patterns, and none cultivates unusual colour types so assiduously. In very recent times, yet another specific colouring, the chocolate-coloured coat of the Rocky Mountain pony, has been added to the Pintos, Palominos, Albinos and Appaloosas.

All these stemmed from those first Spanish horses and so, too, did the 'exotic' gaited horses, now lost to Europe, such as the Fox Trotters and the Walking Horses, as well as the equally spectacular, but nonetheless practical, Peruvian Paso.

RIGHT: *The Rocky Mountain Pony, noted for the smoothness of its gait and striking chocolate coat colour, is a modern American breed.*
BELOW: *The Appaloosa was developed from early Spanish horses and bred selectively by the Nez Perce Indians living in Idaho.*

The Saddlebred

The trio of North American gaited horses – the Saddlebred, the Tennessee Walking Horse and the Missouri Fox Trotter – appear artificial in the extreme to most horse people, a view that is reinforced by the high-set, nicked tails, the long feet, specialist shoes and training aids, which are often considered to be less than humane.

It is largely because of its show-ring image that the American Saddlebred Horse Association refers to its brilliant, extravagantly moving horse as 'America's most misunderstood breed'.

In the show-ring, where the breed competes in three- and five-gaited classes, as well as in harness, there is certainly an element of artificiality. In fact the Saddlebred, like the other members of the specialist, gaited trio, began as an essentially practical animal that satisfied the day-to-day needs of the Southern, plantation-owning gentry, as well as their sense of aesthetic appreciation. In many respects it is still a practical horse. With its feet trimmed normally, it can be used most satisfactorily for straightforward private driving or as a pleasure or trail horse. It is claimed that the Saddlebred can cut cattle, jump well, follow hounds or compete in dressage competitions, and that, despite its natural fire, it is most docile and co-operative.

For all that, it is still best known for its special gaits. In the ring, the breed is shown in either the three- or five-gaited divisions. The former involves the horse at walk, trot and canter, each gait being performed with high action, and in a slow, collected manner which is said to be most comfortable. The five-gaited horse, always shown with a full mane and tail, performs the slow gait and the rack, in addition to the three basic gaits. The slow gait is a four-beat, prancing movement, executed with snap, and with a moment of suspension between each footfall. The rack is the full-speed 'flashy, four-beat gait free from any lateral movement or pacing'. It is exciting to watch, exhilarating to ride, and very fast, a mile (1.5km) being covered in something less than 2 minutes 20 seconds.

LEFT: *The Saddlebred in action and without the customary long feet and heavy shoes.*

TOP: *Even in repose, the Saddlebred, pride of the American show-rings, is a distinctive horse that displays great presence.*

ABOVE: *The Morgan is another all-American product. The breed descends from one prepotent sire, Justin Morgan, after whom it is named.*

The breed evolved during the nineteenth century in the Blue Grass country of Kentucky, and was at first called the Kentucky Saddler. It was the result of selective breeding based on the Narragansett Pacer, a now-extinct American breed which was possibly a cross between imported English horses retaining the ambling gait, and the Spanish-based Indian ponies. The Kentucky Saddler was small, very smooth moving, and noted for its swift and easy pacing gait. Crosses were made to the

Morgan horse and to the all-important Thoroughbred, and, in a remarkably short time, an elegant, utility horse of fixed character and distinctive movement was produced to meet the needs of the day.

In the early years, it took its turn at farm work, carried a man comfortably and in considerable style during the longest working day, and would also double-up as a smart carriage horse.

Every year 4-5,000 Saddlebreds are registered with the breed society.

The Tennessee Walker

Less well known are the Tennessee Walker and the Missouri Fox Trotter; both belong to the same American gaited horse tradition.

The Walker is a large-boned horse, much plainer than the Saddlebred, and with a less elevated action. It originated as a plantation horse in the state of Tennessee during the nineteenth century. Its job was to carry a rider very comfortably for long periods of time, employing three smooth gaits ranging from a swift, flat walk to a much quicker, running walk, and an absolute armchair, rocking-horse canter. In the early days, it was called a Southern Plantation Walking Horse or, more familiarly, a Walker or Turn-Row horse, earning this name for its ability to turn up and down the plantation rows without damaging the young plants.

The Walker is again based on the Narragansett Pacer, and thereafter on a careful amalgam of Thoroughbred, Standardbred, Morgan and Saddlebred blood. The foundation sire of the breed is Black Allan, a Standardbred who was a failure as a harness racer because of his strange walking pace, a peculiarity that he handed down faithfully to his descendants.

Both the walk-gaits of the breed are in four-time, with the head nodding distinctively in time with the movement and the hind feet over-tracking the imprint of the forefeet. The running walk is the most distinctive, and average speeds of 6-9 mph (9-14kph) can be maintained over long distances without the rider being disturbed by the movement in any way. The front foot touches the ground just before the opposite diagonal hind foot, the hind feet over-stepping by as much as 6-15 inches (15-38cm). The resultant gliding motion is accompanied by the characteristic head nodding, rhythmically swinging ears, and, at top speed, clicking teeth! The gaits are said to be in-bred, and impossible to teach.

Today's Walking Horse, and there are some quarter of a million of them, is both a show and a pleasure horse. 'Ride one today and you'll own one tomorrow', is the claim of the Walking Horse Breeders' Association, and many people do just that. The gliding, 'bounce-free' gait, and the horse's reputation as the most reassuring mount for the novice or nervous rider, ensure its popularity.

The Missouri Fox Trotter

The Missouri Fox Trotter comes from the Ozark Hills of Missouri and Arkansas, and is an older breed, established about 1820, derived from interbreeding between Morgans, Thoroughbreds and horses of predominantly Spanish Barb ancestry, which are sometimes wrongly referred to as Arab. In-breeding produced a fixed type of utility horse suited to the rough ground conditions of the region and acceptable, despite the comfort of the ride, to the area's puritanical religious sects, which had outlawed racing as sinful.

The objective was a strong, enduring horse that would adapt to the ground and could be ridden for long stretches at speed without tiring himself or his rider.

The result is a compact, plain horse, moving smoothly in a unique and characteristic gait called the Fox Trot. It is a broken gait, and the horse is exceptionally sure-footed. In simple terms, the horse walks very actively with the forelegs while trotting behind, the hindfeet stepping down and sliding over the tracks of the forefeet. The sliding action minimizes any concussive effect, and the rider is carried without being aware of the movement. The Fox Trot can be maintained for long distances over rough ground at speeds of 5 and 8 mph (8-12kph), and, over short distances, speeds of 10 mph (16kph) can be reached. The head, like that of the Walker, nods in time to the movement, and the tail bobs rhythmically.

The other gaits are the four-time walk, executed with distinct overstriding of the hindfeet, and the canter, a gait between the fast, long-rein lope of the cow pony and the high, slow gait of the Walker and Saddlebred. The Fox Trotter does not have the elevated action of the other two, and the breed society prohibits the use of artificial training aids. There are now well over 15,000 registered Fox Trotters.

FAR LEFT: *The Tennesse Walker has a unique gliding action, accompanied, when travelling at speed, by an audible clicking of the teeth!*

BELOW: *The Missouri Fox Trotter, along with the related Tennessee Walker, is one of the most comfortable horses in the world to ride.*

The South American Paso

Even more specialized is the hardy little Paso of South America, which originates in Peru, although it is also bred in Colombia, and has an enthusiastic following in the States, particularly in California.

The early Spanish horses which came to Peru with Pizzaro may very well have had the ambling gait of the jennet, but that latent ability has been developed and perfected by hundreds of years of highly selective breeding. The result is a distinctive, very specialized riding horse, capable of great endurance and with a unique gait which is now regarded as a breed characteristic. Although the Paso is well able to canter, it rarely does so, preferring what has become its natural gait. It is this characteristic that distinguishes the Paso from the other South American horse, the Criollo, which, like the Paso, originated from the early Spanish imports. It seems possible, however, that these breeds, though undoubtedly of Spanish descent, may have been from strains carrying more of the blood of the Barb, the horse of the North African coastal strip. The Paso is often said to be three-quarters Barb and to have one quarter Spanish blood.

The Paso evolved as a sure-footed, inherently sound horse which was able to carry a man in comfort, and at a very respectable speed, on long-distance journeys over the vast plains and high, rough mountain passes.

The Paso (the word means 'step') has a four-beat *lateral* gait, the *paso* in fact, which is quite unlike any other. The forelegs are thrown out in an arc to the side, like the arms of a swimmer, while the hindlegs move straight to the front, taking very long strides. The quarters are lowered and the hocks brought as far under the body as their construction allows. This combination of loose, flowing foreleg movement and the powerful driving action of the hindlegs gives an exceptionally smooth ride, and can be maintained for long periods of time.

There are, in fact, three carefully preserved divisions within the gait. They are all natural and spring from the same base, and no artificial aids are used in producing them to near perfection.

There is the normal, easy travelling gait, the *Paso Corto*, and the *Paso Fino*, the display or parade gait, which is slow, highly elevated, very collected, and the most brilliant of the three. Finally, there is the *Paso Largo*, an extended gait which can reach speeds of up to 16mph (25kph) over relatively short distances.

ABOVE: *The incredibly tough Criollo is a descendant of the early imports of Spanish ambling horses and may have played some part in the Paso's development.*
FAR LEFT: *The Paso of South America, often called the Peruvian Paso, is another descendant of the Spanish horses. Its unique gait is the result of hundreds of years of selective breeding.*

Coloured horses

Other American favourites include the colour breeds, such as the golden Palomino and the spotted Appaloosa. These colours, and others, occur elsewhere in the world and the horses concerned can hardly be considered breeds in the proper sense, with the sole exception of the Appaloosa. They are, in reality, types rather than breeds, because the characteristics of height, conformation etc. are not fixed. In America, however, they are accorded breed status, and are fully documented.

The Palomino colouring is found in a variety of breeds from Welsh ponies to Saddlebreds, although it does not occur in the pure-bred Arab or the Thoroughbred. The first Palomino in America was probably introduced in the early sixteenth century. Indeed, it has been suggested that the name Palomino is derived from a Spanish Don, Juan de Palomino, who received a horse of this colour from Cortes. Other suggestions are that the name is taken from the name of a golden Spanish grape, or from *paloma*, the Spanish word for dove. In Spain they are often called Ysabella, after Queen Isabella who encouraged their breeding.

The Palomino Horse Association Inc. was formed in 1936 'for the perpetuation and improvement of the Palomino horse through the recording of bloodlines and the issue of certificates of registration to qualifying horses'. It defines the ideal colour as being that of a newly minted gold coin, with a pure white mane and tail.

Even the Albino, which in Europe would be considered as having an unfortunate congenital deficiency of colouring pigment in the skin and hair, has a breed society, and even a foundation sire, Old King of the White Horse Ranch in Naper, Nebraska. The breed society, The American White Horse Club, divides its entries into Cremes and Whites, and in both instances encourages animals that are of Arab type. The requirements for a White are a snow-

TOP LEFT: *An Appaloosa with a 'blanket' marking – one of the five accepted patterns.*
CENTRE LEFT: *The coat colour of the Palomino should be that of a newly minted coin.*
BELOW LEFT: *A North American Pinto with the characteristic 'tobiano' (skewbald) marking.*

white coat, mane and tail, and pink skin, with eyes either brown, dark blue, hazel or light blue. Wall eyes, where the white of the eye is clearly visible, are not uncommon in Albinos.

The Appaloosa, on the other hand, is a distinctive breed, even though the spotted gene is as old as the equine race, and is distributed in every corner of the world. The spotted coat pattern was, indeed, known and esteemed for thousands of years before Columbus sailed for America.

The American version of the spotted horse was developed by the Nez Percé Indians in the eighteenth century, using spotted Spanish stock as a foundation. They lived in the north-east of Oregon, and their lands included fertile, sheltered river valleys, one of which was that of the Palouse river – the name Appaloosa is a corruption of the latter.

The Indians were skilful, selective horse-breeders, and regarded the colour as an attraction as well as a means of camouflage. There are five accepted Appaloosa coat patterns: Leopard, Snowflake, Blanket, Frost and Marbleized. The mane and tail are characteristically short and sparse, and the hooves have black and white vertical stripes. Mottled skin is noticeable around the muzzle and the dock, and there is a white sclera, or membrane, to the eye.

In 1876 the Nez Percé and their horses were virtually wiped out, as the American government pursued a policy of seizing tribal lands. The breed, however, was revived when the Appaloosa Horse Club was formed in 1938, and it now has the third-largest breed registry in the world.

The Indians also favoured the Pinto for its unusual colouring, and these particoloured horses were very popular with the Western cowboy. The Pinto Horse Association, formed in 1956, recognized the Pinto as a breed in 1963 – a period so short that it has to be a world record.

Coloured horses are enormously popular as 'parade' horses and no country makes more use of them than America.

TOP RIGHT: *The 'leopard' markings of this Appaloosa are quite different from those of the 'blanket'-marked horse shown opposite.*
RIGHT: *The colourful Pinto, which today is a popular 'parade' horse, was much favoured by both the Indians and the Western cowboys.*

GO WEST

The Spanish settlers brought with them to the New World a tradition of cattle ranching, finding the great plains ideally suited to support large numbers of cattle. The earliest ranching enterprises were in Mexico and Argentina, and, initially, the end product was not meat but leather. By the nineteenth century, however, the pressures of increasing populations and the rapidly growing process of industrialization that was taking place in both Europe and America, shifted the emphasis to the provision of beef in quantity. As a result of the new demand, cattle ranching spread rapidly into the western United States, while Argentina became the principal supplier of beef to Britain, and to a lesser degree to other European countries.

Cattle ranching on this scale involved the use of a great many horses trained in the techniques of cattle herding, and it needed men with special skills; tough, resourceful men, who were able to cope with the inevitable hardships of the long cattle trails. Around them grew the legend and mythology of the American West, created first by novelists, and then assiduously cultivated by the Hollywood movie, a *genre* that has become one of the great phenomena of the twentieth century. The Western is the modern morality play, in which good always triumphs over evil, and it still retains its appeal.

The reality was less romantic, and not at all heroic. Life was hard, and the Western cowboy had to develop not only special skills, but also a whole range of practical equipment, related directly to the needs imposed by a big, empty country, where a man on foot stood little chance of survival.

RIGHT: *Gold Canyon Ranch, Phoenix, Arizona is a popular venue for a real Western holiday.*
BELOW: *The steer-wrestling event at the world-famous Calgary Stampede.*

The early cowboys

Most of the horses used in the early days of the Western cowboy were the mustangs, or wild crosses of the original Spanish stock. They were not beautiful, but they were agile, tough and wiry specimens, although few stood much over 14 hands high. A cowboy might break his own horse to saddle, but most were broken in rough and ready manner by 'bronco-busters' who made their living that way. Many of the mustangs were wild customers to handle, and breaking them was a matter of staying in the saddle and riding out the bucks and leaps until the animal was too tired to continue the fight. Then the horses had to learn how to work cattle, and acquire the skills upon which the life and limb of the rider would depend. These horses were not much different from the Indian ponies, but sometimes better types could be obtained from the tribes who understood selective breeding and, like the Nez Percé, reared horses like the Appaloosa, known then as the 'Palouse horse'.

Such horses were much prized, for they were stronger and much faster than the average Indian pony. On occasions, the cowboys would have to rope and herd cattle

ABOVE AND ABOVE RIGHT: *The most dangerous of the rodeo events is bare-back riding. The horse's head is free and the cowboy must stay on for the mandatory eight seconds with the help of nothing more than a hand loop.*

BELOW: *The real thing. Working ranch horses are still used in Nevada to move and round up cattle. A good cow pony is highly schooled and will work almost instinctively with the minimal signals from its rider.*

at full gallop, often over rough, mountainous country, and then a fast, sure-footed horse was essential.

After the Civil War (1861-65), better, stronger horses became available; a necessity because of the introduction of heavier cattle and the opening up of the rugged ranges of the north-west. Among these were the Quarter Horses, which were, without doubt, the finest cattle horses in the world. Strong and very agile, they developed innate skills, working cattle instinctively, like sheepdogs with a flock of sheep.

The cowboy ('*vaquero*', 'cowpuncher', 'hand' or 'buckaroo'), whether he came from Texas or California, preferred to ride geldings, which were considered more reliable than mares. The favourite gait, and the most comfortable, was the lope; an easy, relaxed canter with the rein loose and the head carried naturally. The Western horse also jogs in the same relaxed way on a loose rein. The cowboy, riding with long stirrup leathers, never rose to the trot. Riding at a steady jog, a man could travel about five miles (8km) in an hour, while at the lope the speed would increase to between six and eight miles (9.5-13km) an hour. Each rider would have a string of several horses, and on a round-up ('rodeo' or 'cow hunt') would use three or more during the day.

The elite of the *remuda* (the herd of broken ranch horses) was the cutting horse, the best of which were Quarter Horses. Their job was to 'cut' a designated steer from the milling herd, and they did so with extraordinary proficiency, blocking the animal's moves to escape with lightning-quick reactions. Equally prized was the roping horse, which would place the rider in the best position from which to throw his lariat, brace itself against the struggling animal, and keep the rope taut even when the rider dismounted. These highly schooled horses worked almost instinctively, obeying the minimal signals of the reins or the rider's legs.

A 'night horse' was chosen for its steadiness and its ability to work in the dark, and had also to be very sure-footed in the event of a night-time stampede.

TOP RIGHT: *The supreme cow pony is America's most popular breed, the Quarter Horse.*
RIGHT: *The favourite Western gait, the lope. The head is held naturally on a loose rein.*

Western tack and equipment

When the Spanish settled in America they brought with them not only horses, but also their equipment, as well as the methods of schooling that had been developed on the Iberian Peninsula during 700 years of Moorish occupation.

Theirs was the overriding influence in the design of saddles and bridles, and in the training of horses. It provided a foundation that could be adapted to the practical requirements of the ranching industry, which represented the reality of the Western school of horsemanship.

The original cowboy was a specialist, and very conscious of his skills. He worked with a horse and rope, and would not demean himself by 'sod-busting', carrying hay or milking a cow. His clothing and equipment were just as specialized, and if it was sometimes ornamented with silver inlays and the like, it was, nonetheless, practical in every way.

There were, of course, differences in the rigs and accessories employed from one part of the vast cow-country to another, the principal one being between the Texan and the Californian. The Texan, for instance, made use of the 30-40ft (9-12m) lariat ('riata' or 'lasso') of manila rope, while the Californian threw a 'big loop' with a 60-65ft (18-20m) rawhide rope.

Saddles varied in design according to preference and district, additions and refinements being made as circumstances dictated. They all derived from the saddle of the *conquistadores*, inherited by the Mexican *vaquero*, the West's first cattle ranchers. The characteristic horn on the Western saddle was added to act as a post to which the lariat could be tied. Until its appearance in the early nineteenth century, when roping techniques were being developed, one end of the lariat was tied to the horse's tail, a practice that quickly proved to be impractical.

The Western ranching saddle was really a work platform, and was designed to meet all the needs of the range rider. It was broad and heavy, often weighing as much as 40-50lb (18-23kg), but because of the enlarged skirts, this weight, and that of the rider, was

ABOVE: *A practical, no-frills range saddle, which provides a working platform for the cowboy. Instead of stirrup leathers, the cowboy uses wide fenders, which protect the legs from chafing and the horse's sweat. A blanket or a thick pad is always used underneath these broad and heavy Western saddles.*
LEFT: *A more intricately tooled and decorated parade saddle, which, nonetheless, retains the essential features of the working saddle.*
BELOW: *Working range horses in the corral of a Tucson ranch. This group of Appaloosas are wearing simple hackamore bridles, which exert pressure on the nose.*

spread evenly over a large area of the horse's back, thus reducing the likelihood of sores caused by weight being concentrated over one part. As a further protection, the saddle was put on over a heavy, folded blanket, which doubled as a bed-roll for the rider, who, on round-ups and so on, slept rough under the stars.

The Western saddle was very comfortable for long journeys and hard days spent overseeing the herds, and it was designed so that all the cowboy's gear could be securely attached to it.

Instead of the narrow European stirrup leather, the pioneers of the Western saddle introduced fenders, wide pieces of stout leather which protected the rider's clothes from being soaked with sweat, and

prevented his legs being chafed. The width and weight of the fenders ensured that the stirrups which were attached to them moved very little – an advantage when mounting in a hurry. The stirrups themselves were large and heavy, and were made with varying widths of sole supports. They were made of wood covered with rawhide, rather than metal, which would have done nothing to keep the feet warm in cold weather.

In rough, scrub country the Mexican *tapaderos*, leather stirrup hoods, provided both protection and extra warmth, particularly if they were lined with sheepskin in winter.

In California horses were schooled to a very high standard, using the rawhide noseband called *jáquima* (hackamore),

ABOVE: *A typical Texan working cow pony, ridden on the looping rein of the Western horseman and moving in excellent balance.*

before ever a bit was put in the mouth. Thereafter, the horse could be ridden on no more than the weight of the looping rein attached to the curb bit. The same system was used in Texas and Arizona, but conditions were different there and instead of the beautifully made Californian bit, decorated with gold and silver, a plainer curb bit was used, with the cheeks bent backwards to allow the horse to graze. For that reason it was known as a 'grazing' bit.

Open reins were used, and horses were trained to stand still when the rider dismounted and dropped the reins.

Western clothing

The cowboy's clothes were just as suited to his work as his horse and saddle. On his head he wore a broad-brimmed hat, which in time became known as a Stetson, after its principal manufacturer, John Batterson Stetson. It fulfilled a variety of purposes. It was a protection against the sun, and in winter could be tied down to cover the ears. It made a useful water scoop from which to drink, and it was big enough to wave at a wandering steer during herding.

Round his neck, the cowboy tied a cotton bandana. It was possible to filter water through it, it could be used as a mask against the dust, or it would serve as a bandage. He wore a flannel shirt, with a loose vest or short jacket of either cloth or buckskin. His trousers were close-fitting, and possibly reinforced with leather until the advent of denims or Levis. These low-hipped, narrow-legged trousers with flat, non-twisting seams were invented and marketed by a Jewish tailor from New York called Levi Strauss.

The cowboy paid particular attention to his boots, and paid a lot of money for them, too. They were strong, half-length boots of very soft leather, usually made to measure, and perhaps decorated with intricate tooled designs. Most importantly, they had high, forward-sloping heels which could be dug into the ground to give extra purchase when holding on to a roped calf. The spurs, frequently ornamented ones, for even working cowboys liked to be snappy dressers, were large, heavy, and fitted with blunt, loose rowels which jangled as their owner rode round the wary cattle, and gave warning of his presence.

In the mesquite country of the Texas range, which was full of strong, thorny scrub, a pair of stout leather chaps (*chaparajos*) with fringed outer seams were essential protective clothing. On the more open range of California, chaps were also an essential item of equipment, but they were often made of sheepskin, or even fur, with pronounced decoration.

LEFT: *A 'cow-girl' in Western gear, which, though colourful, is still essentially practical. The broad-brimmed Stetson protects her face from the sun and rain.*

Most cowboys had a pair of stout, cuffed leather gloves. They kept the hands warm in the bitter winters that were commonplace in Nevada and Wyoming, but, even more importantly, they prevented them being skinned by rope-burns when a steer fought hard against the restraining lariat.

BELOW: *A scene from a typical Hollywood Western. The Texan, on the left, rides an Andalucian horse. His companion is dressed in the traditional style of the Mexican vaquero.*
BOTTOM: *The cowboy places great reliance on his horses, which, surrounded by milling cattle, must remain calm, clever and agile.*

The rodeo

The cowboy's skills are no longer essential in the cattle business, but today they are central to a modern entertainment industry, the competitive rodeo. Rodeos began as informal contests on round-ups, and developed as the main feature of public fairs throughout the West, and then all over the continent. The first one, or the first to charge admission, was held at Prescott, Arizona in 1888. A hundred or so years later, there were more than 700 rodeos being held in America and Canada, under the auspices of the Professional Rodeo Cowboys' Association, a body formed in 1936. Prize money is big, amounting to over $16 million, and is competed for by some 5,500 full members, and 3,500 permit-holders, the apprentices of the sport who must earn $2,500 a year before being admitted to full membership. The top event, apart from the famous Calgary Stampede, is the annual National Finals Rodeo, now held at Las Vegas and formerly in Oklahoma. Prize money at the Finals is in excess of $2 million. The sport's most coveted title is that of World Champion All-Round Cowboy, and is awarded to the rider winning the most prize money in the year in a variety of events .

Many of the rodeo competitors are professionals, travelling widely round the national circuit, intent on amassing World Championship points and considerable sums of money. Others are weekend performers competing locally.

There are now six basic competitive events: saddle-bronc riding, bareback riding, bull riding, steer wrestling, calf roping, and team roping, as well as rodeo games, such as barrel racing, pole bending and chuck-wagon racing.

The 'classic' rodeo event is saddle-bronc riding. It is the most difficult, but is, surprisingly, the least dangerous, and serious injuries are rare. The horse, wearing a saddle, and a bucking strap round the loins, as well as a headcollar and rope, is mounted while in a chute. When the horse is released and comes bucking out of the chute, the rider has to stay on board for eight seconds, while being marked for the style of the ride, based on the synchronization of the rider's body movements with those of the horse. The animals are often purpose-bred for the rodeo, and, like the riders, 'compete' for special awards. There are, for instance, titles such as Saddle-Bronc of the Year, Bareback Horse of the Year and so on.

Bareback riding is nearly as difficult as saddle-bronc riding, but very much more dangerous. The horse has its head quite free, and the rider has nothing more than a hand-loop, fastened to a surcingle or cinch, to help him stay on. 'Style' – the horse being spurred by the lower legs swinging back and forth – is a deciding factor, and, once more, the rider must sit out the powerful bucks and plunges for the mandatory eight seconds.

Bull riding is a great attraction for spectators and is judged in a similar way. The greatest danger comes when the rider falls off, and that is when the services of the bullfighters are required, to distract the attention of the enraged animal.

Two riders are needed for steer wrestling, although only one competes. The other, the 'hazer', positions the steer so that the competing cowboy can jump on to the animal and bring it down. The event is decided on time, and in most instances the steer is down in three or four seconds.

For calf roping there is no horse superior to the Quarter Horse, the breed that dominates the Western events. The calf is roped, the horse holds the rope taut while the rider dismounts and hog-ties the calf. Once again, the contest is judged on time.

Team roping involves two riders, one to act as the 'header', who lassos the steer round the head or horns, and the other, the 'heeler', who ropes the steer's heels.

BELOW LEFT: *One of the rodeo events in a lighter vein is the chuck-wagon race, which is probably not much different from, and no less dangerous than, the chariot races that were a central feature of the Roman circus. To drive a team at full gallop on an oval track requires a lot of skill and just as much nerve.*

ABOVE: *The moment of truth as the cowboy grapples with the steer in an attempt to bring it down. The event is decided on time; it usually takes three or four seconds.*
BELOW: *Calf roping is one of the classic rodeo classes. In these events, no horse is superior to the intelligent Quarter Horse.*

ABOVE: *Barrel racing, involving very tight turns, is fast and very exciting to watch.*
BELOW: *The supreme, and most difficult, event of the rodeo is saddle-bronc riding. The horse is encouraged to buck hard by the bucking strap round its loins and the rider is marked on the 'style' of the ride over eight seconds.*

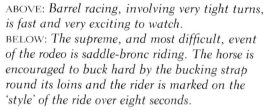

PONY PARADE

By modern definition, the horses of prehistory were in fact ponies, because of their size. Subsequently, equines developed largely in accordance with their environment, and the accelerating intervention of man practising selective breeding and hand-feeding.

It is obvious enough that equines evolving in mountainous regions, which were subject to climatic extremes and had only minimal vegetation, would be small in stature, offering the smallest possible body surface area. These smaller, mountain-dwelling equines were naturally hardy and constitutionally equipped to cope with the harsh rigours of their habitat. What is not always readily appreciated by many modern horse-lovers is that they also developed particular pony characteristics that are different from those of the horse.

It has been customary to fix an arbitrary division between horses and ponies by height. Animals over 15 hands high are termed horses, and those under this size are ponies. This is convenient for practical purposes, but takes no account of the proportions and special character of ponies, in relation to horses, which make the essential difference between the two.

A great number of Arabs are, indeed, below the 15 hands mark, but they have the proportions of a horse, and are never referred to as ponies. Even the tiny Caspian and the dwarf Falabella are really of horse character. The case of the polo pony is not quite the same. Until the height limit was abandoned early this century, the polo pony was indeed a pony of under 14.2 hands, and, in England, was often the progeny of native pony mares, Dartmoors, New Forests and so on, crossed with small Thoroughbreds. Today, the modern polo pony stands at around 15.2 hands high, and is a small horse.

True ponies are to be found all over the world, and are the most fascinating and attractive animals. However, the most significant grouping, of no less than nine established breeds, is represented by the Mountain and Moorland breeds native to Britain. There are other pony breeds, of course, but none approach the British ones in variety, or in their potential as riding and driving ponies, and as a valuable basis for cross-breeding.

RIGHT: *A pair of appealing Welsh pony foals at play in the sunshine.*
BELOW: *The size of the tiny Falabella can be judged by the height of the daffodils.*

Mountain and Moorland

The unique group that makes up the British native pony breeds exists because of the isolation of the British Isles following the Ice Age, when they were cut off from mainland Europe. The last land-bridge, from the Scilly Isles, disappeared around 15000 BC, in the Old Stone Age, and no new additions to the British equine population were made for the next 14,000 years. From the Bronze age, approximately 1000 BC, there were ships big enough to carry horses and cattle, and, from that time, there is evidence of horses being brought to Britain from Scandinavia and Iceland. Almost certainly, the Shetland originally came from those countries, but much earlier. Its diminutive stature was fixed by the isolation of its habitat, which also prohibited the use of outside crosses.

Dales, Fells and Highlands would all have benefited from stock of Scandinavian origin, and it was not until the Roman occupation that significant infusions of Oriental blood were made to much of the indigenous stock, as the Phoenician traders brought in Eastern horses on the Western trading routes.

The title Mountain and Moorland arises because the original habitats of all the nine breeds native to the British Isles were the wild uplands, beginning in the south-west with Dartmoor and Exmoor, continuing up the western side of the country through the mountainous areas of Wales, and so northwards to the dales and fells along the Pennine Chain. In Scotland, ponies inhabited the Western Isles and Shetland, as well as the mainland. The rough, inhospitable land of Connemara, in the far west of Ireland, supported its own remarkable breed, and yet another race of ponies, more affected by outside influence, found a living in the New Forest of Hampshire, the ancient hunting ground of Kings, and still the largest parcel of unenclosed land in southern England.

LEFT: *These are typical examples of the smaller Welsh Cobs, the Welsh ponies of Cob type, Section C, which do not exceed 13.2hh.*
RIGHT: *A Connemara mare and foals at grass. Their original habitat was the wild and inhospitable Western seaboard of Ireland.*

Today, although there are no more truly feral stocks, ponies still inhabit these areas. They are, of course, also bred at studs throughout Britain, as well as elsewhere in the world, for there is a market for all the British breeds in countries as far apart as Scandinavia and Australasia.

Obviously, all the breeds have been improved, and even 'modernized', by out-crossing and selective breeding over a long period of time. However, they still retain a distinct character and appearance, and they certainly have not lost the hardiness, soundness of constitution, and sagacity derived from their original environment. They have the ability to survive, and flourish, on the most sparse feed, and they have qualities which would seem to reflect the natural vigour of their primitive ancestors – a vigour not so evident in so many of the 'invented' horse breeds.

Although the native strains are very old, the concept of 'breeds' as such is a modern one. Today's pony breeds can be said to date from the establishment of the breed societies, and the introduction of Stud Books. The first Stud Book was that of the Shetland, opened in 1890, only a hundred years ago. The rest all belong to the present century, the Dartmoor Pony Society being formed as late as 1924 following the demise of an earlier association.

The Exmoor

The oldest of the British native breeds is the Exmoor, and apart from the 'primitive' horses, the Tarpan and the Asiatic Wild Horse, it is probably as old as any other in the world. Its principal ancestor was the first of four equine types of pre-domestication, Pony Type 1 referred to in *In the Beginning* (see page 11). Remains of that primeval forebear have been found in Alaska, and the Exmoor still retains some similar features. The jaw formation, for example, is peculiar, because of a seventh molar found in no other equine.

Its natural habitat is the isolated Exmoor moorland in south-west England, where herds are still run out all year, being brought in annually for inspection. Although it stands at about 12.2 hands high, the Exmoor is so strongly built and well-balanced that it is quite capable of carrying a grown man for a full day's hunting over the Moor. There is some evidence of Spanish or Barb blood being introduced to Exmoor early in the last century, but although efforts have been made to improve the breed with outcrosses, they have never been successful. Today, ponies bred away from the Moor quickly lose type, and breeders find it necessary to return to the Moor stock to maintain the pony's original character.

The Exmoor is unmistakable in its appearance because of the mealy colouring on the muzzle, round the eyes, and on the underside of the body. It has no white markings. The eyes, called 'toad' eyes, are hooded to provide protection against the weather, and the Exmoor's tail has an extra fan-like growth at the top, an 'ice' tail, for the same purpose. In winter it also grows a double-textured waterproof coat.

Dartmoor and New Forest ponies

In the south and the south-west of England, the neighbours of the Exmoor are the Dartmoor and the New Forest. Both have been much influenced by other breeds because of their geographical situation, and, even today, the New Forest is less fixed in type than other native breeds. For all that, two remarkable breeds have emerged. The Dartmoor is now a wonderfully graceful riding pony of up to 12.2 hands, with pronounced jumping ability. It owes a great deal to the early polo stallions, and, though few ponies are now bred on the Moor, the breed is established in its own right throughout Europe, and crosses very well with Thoroughbreds and Arabians to produce a bigger pony.

Similarly, many of the best New Forest ponies are bred outside their natural environment. Nonetheless, they retain their character and are probably, with the Connemara of Ireland (see page 111) as commercially viable as any pony breed. At 14.2 hands high, the New Forest has all the scope and ability to compete in the major junior disciplines, and it can be ridden by adults and teenagers alike.

BELOW LEFT: *Britain's oldest native pony and one of the world's most ancient breeds is the Exmoor, which inhabits the moorlands of south-west England. It is unmistakeable on account of the mealy colouring of its muzzle.*
BELOW: *The modern Dartmoor is a splendid riding pony with good jumping ability and an exceptional action.*
BOTTOM: *Wild New Forest ponies can still be seen grazing unconcernedly on the roadside verges. The best, however, are stud-bred.*

The Shetland

Almost as old as the Exmoor pony is the Shetland, the smallest of the native breeds, with an original habitat on the bleak, treeless Shetland Isles, to the north-east of Scotland. There is little vegetation to provide food, which is one reason for the pony's small stature, but, in relation to its size, this is one of the world's most powerful equines. It can, in fact, carry a man nimbly, and is well able to work under the heavy weight of panniers loaded with peat. Unlike other equines, whose height is calculated in the medieval measurement of a 'hand' (4in/10cm), the Shetland is always measured in inches, the average height at the wither being about 40in (1 metre). A special feature is the extra large nasal cavity, which allows the air to warm before entering the lungs. This construction is common in equines from the northern latitudes, but also occurs in the Exmoor.

Shetlands were once much used as pit ponies. Today they are used as mounts for small children, and for driving, at which they excel. They are popular in circuses, nature parks and so on, and have been exported in large numbers to both America and Canada. Indeed, the Americans have produced their own 'new look' Shetland, by crossing the finer types of Island pony with Hackney ponies, and topping the mixture up with a dash of Arab and small Thoroughbred. The result is, for the most part, a harness pony of pronounced Hackney character, with brilliant action. Otherwise it has little to do with the tough Shetland Island pony.

BELOW: *The Shetland is the smallest of the native breeds, averaging about 40in (1 metre) at the wither, but is very powerful for its size.*

The Highland

The Shetland's neighbour, the powerfully built Highland, which stands at about 14.2 hands high, is the biggest of the native breeds. It, too, is an ancient breed, and usually has the primitive dorsal stripe running down the back, as well, sometimes, as zebra markings round the legs.

Over 400 years ago, French horses, the equivalent of the modern Percheron, were used to upgrade the native highland stock. Later Spanish stock was used, and then, inevitably, the refining Eastern blood, as well as that of the Clydesdale, which increased the weight but was otherwise a less fortunate departure.

The modern Highland, however, remains a versatile all-rounder, as good in harness as under saddle. It is up to weight, very sure-footed, and so kind-tempered that it is the automatic choice of Scotland's booming trekking industry. They also work in forestry, clearing and hauling logs, and they are the only ponies strong enough, and sufficiently unflappable, to carry an 18st (110kg) deer carcass off the hill when the deer herds have to be culled.

Dales and Fell ponies

In northern England there are two genetically related breeds, the Dales and the Fell ponies. It is customary to distinguish between them by saying that the larger Dales Pony is found on the east of the Pennines, in the upper Dales of Tyne, Allen, Wear, and Tees in North Yorkshire, while the Fell occupies the northern edges of the Pennines, and the moorlands of Westmorland and Cumberland on the other side. In fact, both are branches of the same root, and developed according to their uses.

TOP LEFT: *The modern Highland is a powerful pony of about 14.2 hands high. It is docile, versatile and very surefooted.*
CENTRE LEFT: *In the past, the usually black Dales Pony was used as a strong, reliable pack pony. Today it is a notable performer in harness and is also used for trekking.*
BOTTOM LEFT: *The lighter Fell Pony, related to the Dales, is considered more of a riding type, but it, too, goes well in harness.*

The Connemara

The Connemara, 13-14.2 hands high, is just as much a mixture of bloods as the other native breeds, and equally in demand. Arabs, Welsh, Thoroughbreds and Hackneys have all been used in the upgrading process to produce probably the most brilliant performance pony in the world. It is fast, courageous, a natural and remarkable jumper, as well as being hardy and very sound. As a cross for the production of competition horses it is unrivalled.

BELOW: *The Connemara, which can be as big as 14.2 hands high, is much in demand throughout Europe as a top-class performance pony.*

SPORTING HORSES

Competition is as old as the history of man, and from the time when horses were first tamed and began their association with the human race it was inevitable that they would be matched against each other in tests of speed and endurance. Since human nature is unlikely to have changed very much over the centuries, it is highly probable that such races involved the wagering of goods, and later money, by the parties concerned.

Today, racing is classed as a sport, but in reality it is a huge multinational industry in which betting is a central element. There are owners and trainers who do not bet, and jockeys, under the rules of racing, are prohibited from doing so, but there is no doubt that money generated by on- and off-course betting underpins the structure.

The establishment of modern, organized racing was closely associated with the evolution of the Thoroughbred racehorse in England, which began in the seventeenth and eighteenth centuries, and Britain, which even then had a long racing tradition, is responsible for setting the pattern of racing worldwide.

Flat-racing takes place at courses all over the world, but steeplechasing over fences is essentially an English sport. There is, of course, some racing over fences elsewhere in Europe, and there are one or two events in America, but these do not approach the standards and size of the highly organized British 'winter game'.

Polo, although it was played in one form or another as much as 2,500 years ago, is certainly not as old as racing, nor is it

nearly as popular. It is a sport in which betting plays no part, and it is conducted on an organized basis in many countries.

Just as racing revolves around the Thoroughbred horse, so also does the modern game of polo, which uses ponies that are almost wholly Thoroughbred. The game had its origins in the East, but was introduced to Europe, the Americas and Australasia by the British, who brought it back from India in the nineteenth century.

RIGHT: *An evocative picture of Thoroughbred racehorses at early morning exercise on the gallops at Lambourn, one of the most important centres of English racing.*
BELOW: *At St Moritz, racing on the snow is a popular and established sport. The horses are shod with ice nails to prevent slipping.*

'The sport of kings'

The first record of racing in England dates from 1174, in the reign of Henry II, and concerns a race that took place at Smithfield, now within the City of London. Today, despite a not undesirable rationalization within the past 30 years, there are still many more racecourses, and races, in Britain, in relation to the size of the country, than anywhere else in the world. Indeed, anyone living in Britain (with the exception of the northernmost parts of Scotland) is within comparatively easy reach of a racecourse.

There are 59 courses in all; 25 are given over to National Hunt racing over fences, a sport which is followed enthusiastically in Britain, but is not carried on so extensively, if at all, elsewhere in the world. The number of jumping courses is an indicator of the sport's popularity. Of the remaining courses, for instance, 18 are stage meetings under both Flat and National Hunt rules, while 16 are devoted entirely to the crowded flat-racing calendar between March and October. The courses vary in size and facilities, from the fashionable magnificence of Royal Ascot, attended annually during the Royal meeting in June by HM The Queen and members of her family, to the homely, smaller, jumping courses at Bangor-on-Dee or Cartmel.

Ascot racecourse was laid out in 1711, on the initiative of another Royal racing enthusiast, Queen Anne, and British racing has traditionally enjoyed Royal patronage from a very early date, hence its popular title, 'The Sport of Kings'.

James I, who enjoyed both racing and hunting, was responsible for putting Newmarket on the map as the future headquarters of racing, and, in the reign of the ill-fated Charles I, regular spring and autumn meetings were held on the famous Newmarket Heath. After the Restoration of

BELOW: *A string of racehorses exercising in the English countryside. All the stable staff are now required to wear protective helmets.*

114

ABOVE: *Arab horses racing at Kempton Park, one of the courses close to London.*

the monarchy in May 1660, Charles II continued the Royal association with the town, and was largely responsible for its development, building a small Palace there and visiting the town frequently. He also indulged his passion for racing, but did so constructively, often acting as an arbiter in disputes. The King was so keen that he rode in many matches himself. It was he who instituted the famous Newmarket Town Plate in 1665. This four-mile (6.4km) race, open to amateurs, is still held annually on the Round course, all riders having to carry 12st (76kg). King Charles himself rode in the Town Plate, and won the race on two

occasions. The name of the King's favourite black stallion, Old Rowley, is preserved for posterity in racing's best known 1,600m course, Newmarket's Rowley Mile – indeed, the King's amorous adventures earned him the nickname of 'Old Rowley'!

Newmarket today still revolves round the horse, its American equivalent being Lexington in Kentucky's Blue Grass country. Some 50 trainers are based in the town and, at the height of the season, upwards of 2,500 horses are in training at the various yards.

Two of the five English classics are held at Newmarket: the 2,000 Guineas, first run in 1809, and the 1,000 Guineas, for fillies, established in 1814. Both are run over a mile (1.6km) and both take place in April.

The Jockey Club, the governing body of flat-racing in Britain, has its headquarters in Newmarket's High Street, and owns the 4,000 acres (1,600 ha) comprising Newmarket Heath, which include the training gallops and the 2,500 acres (1,000 ha) acres covered by the two racecourses.

Granted a Royal Charter in 1970, the Jockey Club was founded in about 1752 by a group of interested gentry and aristocrats, although it did not publish a list of its members until 1835. Similar organizations now exist in all racing countries.

So far as the horses were concerned, *An Introduction to a General Stud Book* was published by Wetherby's, secretaries to the Jockey Club, in 1791, and the first volume of the Stud Book itself appeared in 1808.

Flat-racing

During the first half of the eighteenth century, the emphasis was on distance races of up to four miles (6.4km) which took the form of several heats followed by a final, a matter which speaks volumes for the stamina of the early Thoroughbred. Far shorter races became the norm in the latter part of the century, and this trend is reflected in the British Classic races for three-year-olds.

The Classic races comprise five events. The St. Leger is run over 1¾ miles (2.8km) in September at Doncaster, where racing has taken place since 1595. Doncaster has the distinction of opening the Flat season with the Lincoln Handicap in March, and closing it with the November Handicap. The St. Leger, named after Colonel St. Leger of Park Hill, was first run in 1776.

The 1,000 and 2,000 Guineas are run at Newmarket, while the Derby and the Oaks, (for fillies only), are run over 1½ miles (2.4km) at the most famous of British courses, Epsom, which is no more than 15 miles (25km) from the centre of London. The history of racing on Epsom Downs dates from the fifteenth century, when Charles II, the Merry Monarch, attended racing there with his court.

The first Derby in 1780, named after the 12th Earl of Derby, was won by Diomed, owned by one of the great pioneering figures of the Turf, Sir Charles Bunbury. The race might well have gone down in history as the Bunbury, for the privilege of naming it was settled by Sir Charles and the Earl on the toss of a coin. The Oaks, the race for fillies, was first run in 1779, and was named after the Earl's Epsom residence. That first race was won by Bridget, owned appropriately by Lord Derby.

The Derby and the Oaks are now run during the Epsom Classic Week in early June. In the nineteenth century, it was customary for Parliament not to sit on Derby day.

TOP LEFT: *Early morning at Churchill Downs, Louisville, USA. The horse in the foreground, in Western tack, acts as an escort.*
LEFT: *Racing on the prestigious Churchill Downs course, where the Kentucky Derby is run. Racing here is on a 'dirt' surface.*

The famous Triple Crown is the composite term given to the 2,000 Guineas, the Derby and the St. Leger. The last winner of the Triple Crown was the great Nijinsky, in 1970.

All countries where racing takes place on an organized basis have their equivalents of the Classics, although not necessarily over the same distances.

In modern times the most influential racing nations, other than Britain, have been France, which dominated the European scene after the Second World War, Italy and, of course, America.

The French influence came largely through the studs owned by the millionaire Marcel Boussac, and stallions like his Tourbillon, Pharis and Asterus; while Italy had a profound effect through the Dormello Stud, owned by the greatest breeding genius of the century, Federico Tesio, whose horses Donatello II, Nearco and Ribot were of enormous importance to the world of racing. Ribot, when leased to the United States, became the world's best Classic sire.

Australia and New Zealand support large and effective racing industries, and both have developed their own type of racehorse.

Racing in America began almost as soon as the first English settlers set foot in the New World and could clear 'race paths' through the brush land. The first racecourse was set out on Long Island, close to the present-day Belmont Park, in 1664 by the first Governor of New York, Richard Nicolls. Today, Thoroughbred breeding is centred on the Blue Grass country of Kentucky, and training is usually carried out on the tracks, many of which are 'dirt-track' courses rather than grass. The Kentucky enterprises probably represent the greatest multi-million dollar industry in the Thoroughbred world.

Initially, America followed the British pattern of four-mile (6.4km) races, but eventually the emphasis was shifted to shorter sprint races for two- and three-year-olds. The Kentucky Derby, for instance, run at Churchill Downs, Louisville, is a quarter of a mile (40m) shorter than the Epsom prototype. Nonetheless, America produces some excellent middle-distance horses, and a lot of American Thoroughbreds have done well in the European classics. The legendary Man O'War, whose statue surmounts his grave at

ABOVE: *Thoroughbred racing takes place all over the world. This picture was taken at the Caymans Park racecourse in Jamaica.*

BELOW: *One of the world's most beautiful racecourses – at Gulf Stream, Miami, Florida. This scene typifies American flat-racing.*

the entrance to the Kentucky Horse Park, Lexington, can still be considered as America's greatest horse (he was generally described as 'the mostest horse'), despite the more recent records of sires like Bold Ruler; Secretariat, winner of the American Triple Crown in 1973; and Seattle Slew, who won it in 1977. Man O'War appears in a host of Classic pedigrees, including those of the Epsom Derby winners, Never Say Die, Sir Ivor and Relco.

The American Classics are the Kentucky Derby, the Preakness Stakes, the Belmont Stakes and the Coaching Club American Oaks, the last two being held at Belmont. The Triple Crown comprises the first three.

Steeplechasing

The spiritual homes of steeplechasing are Britain and Ireland. America's big jumping race is the Maryland Hunt Cup, which is quite different from the great English races. It is held over open country, without the benefit of grandstands and the like, and is run over post-and-rail fences, rather than the more usual brush.

The only European race bearing some resemblance to the English pattern is the Czechoslovakian Gran Pardubice Steeplechase. It is really a cross-country race over four miles (6.4km) and numerous formidable natural obstacles.

The first recorded match, which gave the sport its name, took place in Ireland in 1752, when Messrs O'Callaghan and Blake raced their hunters over the four and a half miles (7km) separating Buttevant Church

ABOVE: *In full cry over the most famous steeplechase course in the world – the Grand National at Aintree, first run in 1837.*
ABOVE LEFT: *A water jump is a feature of English 'chasing' courses. The spread is big but it rarely causes trouble.*
LEFT: *The field close-bunched over one of the Cheltenham fences. The Cheltenham Festival is the Mecca of steeplechasing.*

steeple from St. Leger Church – from steeple to steeple, hence 'steeplechase'.

The most famous of all English 'chases is the Grand National, first run in 1837. It is held at Aintree in March, over a distance of 4 miles 856 yards (7.22km), and includes 30 big, very stout and imposing fences, some of which have formidable drops on the landing side. One of the most famous is Becher's Brook, which has to be jumped twice. It is named after Captain Becher, an early competitor, who fell into it, and it continues to take its toll today.

Just as Newmarket is the centre of flat racing, so Cheltenham and particularly the Cheltenham Festival, is the Mecca of steeplechasing. The most prestigious of the season's events, the Gold Cup (first run in 1924) is held there, as well as the Champion Hurdle (instituted in 1927), the Champion Chase, and a number of the very best races which attract the cream of English and Irish horses.

Britain also has the amateur sport of point-to-pointing; in fact, there are hunt races run by almost every registered hunt in the country, during the season from February to late April or early May. Point-to-points – a misleading name, since they are now run over oval, built-up courses – are for horses that have been hunted with a recognized pack of hounds, and they take place over a minimum of three miles (4.8km) and 18 fences. A dozen or more point-to-point meetings are held every weekend during the season, and are attended by large crowds intent on enjoying a real country sport.

LEFT: *The sport for amateurs is the Hunt point-to-point, which provides as many thrills and spills as the professional game.*

Polo

The first Western contact with polo was made by British soldiers and civilians serving in India in the nineteenth century. They learnt it from the Manipuris, the people of the small state of Manipur, which is between Assam and Burma, and where polo, played on ponies no bigger than about 12.2 hands high, is a national game, with every village having its own team. By 1870, largely as a result of the efforts of John Sherer, later a Major-General, who became known as the Father of Modern Polo, the game was played by the army and civilians at every cantonment throughout British India as well as in the native Indian states.

Polo was first played in England in 1869, as 'Hockey on Horseback', at Aldershot, by officers of the 10th Hussars. A year later the Hussars played against their rivals, the 9th Lancers, at Hounslow with eight players being fielded each side.

The game was introduced to America in 1878, following a visit made two years previously by the newspaper tycoon, James Gordon Bennett Jr. to Hurlingham, the fashionable centre of the English game. Bennett became a liberal patron of the sport, and in 1882 the legendary Meadow Brook Club was formed to become the headquarters of American polo, in the same way as Hurlingham filled that position in respect of the game in England.

Within four years the number of players had been reduced to four each side, and by 1909, when the superbly drilled American team beat the English on their home-ground for the Westchester Cup, international supremacy had moved inexorably to the Americans.

They were, for the most part, mounted on Argentine ponies, and there is no doubt that Argentina was the leading polo nation of the world from the 1930s onwards. Ponies were plentiful, and cheaply produced by natural, professional horsemen. In fact the game was first played in Argentina in 1877, by Englishmen, who

BELOW: *The young entry. Polo being played enthusiastically by members of the Vale of Aylesbury Branch of the Pony Club.*

were responsible for the formation of numerous clubs.

The height limit of 14.2 hands for polo ponies, brought in by the British, was abolished in 1916, largely at the instigation of the Americans, and the average height is now between 15 and 15.3 hands.

Handicapping, on the American system, involves the grading of players from −2 to +10 goals. 'High-goal' polo is when the team aggregate handicap is 19 and above, 'medium-goal' when it is between 15 and 18.

Polo is played at the gallop, and is the fastest game in the world. The object is the simple one of scoring more goals than one's opponents, by hitting a 3in (8cm) diameter willow ball through 10ft (3m) high goalposts placed 24ft (7.3m) apart, with a bamboo mallet, often while travelling at speed. The ground measures 300×200yd (275×180m) and is usually enclosed by low boards.

A match lasts something under an hour, and is divided into *chukkas* of seven and a half minutes duration. A high-goal match is divided into five or six *chukkas*, and a smaller event into four. Ponies are changed after each *chukka*, and no pony plays more than two *chukkas* in a match.

ABOVE: *High-goal polo is regularly staged on the Palm Beach ground and the overall standard of the game in America is high.*

BELOW: *In St Moritz, grounds of ice are no deterrent to keen polo players and championships are held there annually.*

OUT HUNTING

Hunting, whether for food or sport, is elemental to the human condition and today, in terms of hunting the fox and the red deer in Britain and Ireland for instance, it is viewed by many as a means of conservation.

In Britain and Ireland, where hunting is carried out more extensively than in any other countries, there are upwards of 400 packs of hounds, hunting fox, red deer and hare. More than half a million people hunt during the season (foxhunting begins in November and ends in April), and a very sizeable industry revolves around the sport.

Foxhunting is also popular in America and Canada, and has been established in those countries since the eighteenth century, although the quarry in North America, more often than not, is the grey fox, which has a regrettable tendency to climb trees and run in circles.

Both New Zealand and Australia have a hunting tradition. There are no foxes in New Zealand, but there are plenty of harrier (hare-hunting) packs, and in Tasmania the kangaroo, wallaby and deer are all hunted.

On the mainland of Europe, France, which has the oldest tradition of organized hunting and hound breeding, continues to practise *La Grande Vénerie*, that is the pursuit of the Beasts of the Forest – the deer, the wild boar and, in times past, the wolf. The hunting of hare and foxes is termed *La Petite Vénerie*, and is no longer carried on in France and other countries of the European mainland because the disease rabies, which can be carried by foxes, is endemic in those countries.

From the time when the Egyptian Pharaohs and Assyrian Kings hunted the lion from their chariots, hunting has inspired a vast quantity of literature in its praise. Possibly none is so popular, or captures so well the essential hunting spirit, as the work of Robert Smith Surtees (1803-64), the creator of the immortal grocer of Gt. Coram Street, John Jorrocks Esq., Master of Foxhounds.

''Unting', said Jorrocks in one of his 'sportin' lectors', 'is all that's worth living for – all time is lost wot is not spent in 'unting – it's like the hair we breathe – if we have it not, we die – it's the sport of kings, the image of war without its guilt and only five and twenty per cent of the danger.'

RIGHT: *Horses steam as the field waits in a ride through the covert. Over half-a-million people hunt during the English season, which lasts from November to April.*
BELOW: *Be with them I will! A bold hunter jumping well over a respectable-sized hedge.*

The history of the hunt

It was the Norman Conquest of England, in the eleventh century, which introduced *la vénerie française* to Britain and brought rules and science to the hunting of the forest beasts. The acknowledged 'beasts of the chase' eight to nine hundred years ago were the stag, the boar and the hare. The fox was then hardly considered a worthwhile quarry. Hunting then, as now, was by scent, the heavy deep-tongued Gascon, Talbot and St Hubert hounds, with their great scenting ability, providing a link between the mounted followers and their huntsman and the pursued animal. Even today, the language of hunting has its origin in the old Norman-French terms.

Only towards the end of the seventeenth century did the English begin to hunt the fox, which, though classed as vermin, ran straighter and stronger than the hare, and, because its scent was not as powerful as that of the stag, presented a greater challenge to the huntsman. That enigmatic property, scent, has occupied the attention of the experts in the art of venery, or hunting with hounds, for centuries. Scent is exuded from the pads of the fox, and from beneath his *brush* – hunting parlance for the fox's tail – and will vary in its intensity according to the weather.

Staghunting, of course, has an advantage over foxhunting, in that the quarry provides edible meat of high quality. In England the stag was jealously preserved and protected by harsh laws as a royal beast, and was the chosen quarry of the Norman, Plantagenet and Tudor dynasties. Staghunting went into decline largely because of the clearance of the great forests, which were the natural habitat of the deer, and then later in the eighteenth century, because of subsequent improvements in agricultural practice.

Many packs at that time were either disbanded or switched to foxhunting. The famous Duke of Beaufort's Hunt made the change in about 1762. Some packs, however, during the reign of George III (1760-1820), hunted carted stag. The stag was released, and, after sufficient time had been allowed for it to move away, the hounds were put on the line, (the *scent* line). When they caught up with the stag (bringing it 'to bay') it was recaptured unharmed and taken back to its quarters, where it lived in some style, being well fed, until it was needed again. This kind of hunting provided long, fast runs for the mounted followers, and it persisted for a long time. The Norwich Staghounds, the last English pack to hunt carted stag (their's was conveyed to and from the field in its own trailer, and was a great favourite) was disbanded in 1964, when the stag died peacefully of old age, but there are still two Irish packs who follow this form of hunting.

LEFT: *A revival of side-saddle riding has seen many ladies riding in this style with English hunts, and going as well as the men.*

Hunting in France

The hunting of carted stag would find no approval at all in France, where hunting is carried on in its traditional form, with great style and some splendour. There are about 75 packs (*équipage* for the hunting of the stag, *vautrait* where the quarry is the wild boar), and staghunting begins in September, although the season proper opens on November 3. The *boutons* – those members invited by the Master to wear the elaborate hunt livery and decorative buttons

LEFT: *A lady Master in the elaborate and magnificent livery of French hunting sounds a call on the traditional French horn.*
BELOW: *The ritual of the stylized* vénerie française, *far more formal than in England, is strictly observed throughout the long day.*

– turn out in full dress to celebrate St Hubert's Mass and the Blessing of the Hounds, accompanied by grand fanfares on the curled French horns. French hunting, indeed, is a very musical affair, the phases of the chase being attended by numerous appropriate calls, which are compositely titled *fanfares de circonstance.*

The hounds used are noted for their scenting abilities and their tongue (voice), and are usually of the old French strains, *Grand Bleu de Gascogne, Gascon Saintongeais, Française Tricolore* and so on, which have been crossed with English foxhounds to improve their speed and stamina. The ritualized *vénerie française* is regarded as an art and, although the day is a long one, it is very different from an English hunt; no jumping is involved, and horses are selected for their steadiness and stamina, rather than for speed and jumping ability.

English hunts

Three packs in England hunt the red deer: the Devon and Somerset, the Quantock and the Tiverton. Stags are hunted in late summer, autumn and spring, and hinds in mid-winter. The stag to be hunted is located beforehand by the 'harbourer' and on the hunting day it is found and put up by a few, experienced hounds, the 'tufters', before the rest of the pack is put on the line. If the stag is brought to bay, usually in water, it is dispatched at close range with a gun. The hunts, which are integral to the area and the way of life of the rural populace, claim that they perform essential, selective culling of the red deer in the most efficient and humane way, since it is only with hounds that one can dislodge the deer from the thick woodland of the combes, and get within close enough range to

guarantee that the animal is killed outright rather than wounded. For a period during the First World War, hunting stopped on Exmoor and the deer almost disappeared as a result, because of indiscriminate killing.

It is foxhunting, however, that is the most generally practised form of hunting in Britain and Ireland flourish.

Early foxhunting, like other forms of venery at that time, was a slow business, and there was not much evidence of the excitement produced by a run in modern times. Hounds, descended from the heavy French strains, were slow. Their noses were good, and they persevered on the line, making wonderful hound 'music', but there was little opportunity for followers to gallop, and, before the enclosure of agricultural land, nothing to jump either, had such an idea ever occurred to those early sportsmen.

By the second half of the eighteenth century, all that had changed. Hugo

Meynell was hunting the Quorn, the foremost of the English Shire packs, in 1753, and was continually irritated by impatient young thrusters pressing too closely on his hounds. At Brocklesby, the Earl of Yarborough was pioneering the breeding of the English foxhound that combined stamina and nose with speed. The land was being enclosed by every sort of fence; in the English Shires, there were hedges, ditches and stout cattle rails; elsewhere there were stone walls, banks or fearsome dykes. Because of the increasing influence of the Thoroughbred, horses were bigger, more athletic and much faster, and there was no shortage of young bloods to take advantage of those qualities and to pit their skill and courage riding against their

BELOW: *A big field of the Cotswold Hunt moving to the first covert. All members are subject to the authority of the Field-Master.*

peers over the well-fenced Shire country.

Initially, packs of hounds were kept privately, at the expense of the great landowners, men like the Dukes of Beaufort and Grafton, and the Earls of Berkeley, all of whom hunted over vast areas of country. In time, however, as hunting developed and became more popular, and expenses increased, subscriptions were taken from followers to defray the huge costs involved.

The Golden Age of foxhunting is considered to be between 1820 and 1890. The big estates were still intact, there were no cars or motorways, and no petrol fumes to attack the sensitive nostrils of the hounds. Furthermore, the fences were free of wire.

RIGHT: *Galloping on over a big obstacle in the Hurworth Hunt country in North Yorkshire.*
BELOW: *A Christmas card scene as a huntsman takes his hounds on to the meet in a snow-covered countryside.*

Even the Industrial Revolution and the coming of the railways did not have their anticipated effect on the chase. In fact, the railways opened up the country, and made meets more accessible than ever before. Nor could two World Wars in the space of a quarter of a century extinguish the traditional sport of the countryside.

The cream of the English hunting countries (the area covered by a hunt is termed its 'country') lies in the English Midland Shires of Leicestershire, the old county of Rutland, Warwickshire, Northampton and parts of Lincolnshire. The Shire packs are Pytchley, Quorn, Fernie, Belvoir and Cottesmore. For the most part these are undulating 'grass countries', the big pastures being strongly fenced, and they attract large numbers of riders, referred to as 'the field'. The sport is good, hunting is fast, and there is enough jumping to satisfy the most voracious appetite. Not surprisingly, subscriptions to the Shire packs are the highest in the land.

To ride with a Shire pack in full cry requires the very best sort of horse obtainable, not less than three-quarters or seven-eighths Thoroughbred. It must have stamina and boundless courage, be well-made and well-balanced, sound and strong if it is to stand up to the work. It goes without saying that it must gallop and have above-average jumping ability. Furthermore, one such horse will not be enough; two are needed to get through a good day on the grass. It is the custom in the Shires to change horses for the afternoon's business, the second horse being brought up by a 'second-horseman', or, more usually today, driven in a carefully navigated horse-box.

Without doubt, some of the best hunters come out of Ireland, a country with a unique tradition of horsemanship, where so many young horses learn their trade in 'the snaffle and the ashplant' school. Most of them are Irish Draught crosses, that is, the progeny of a Thoroughbred horse put to a roomy Irish Draught mare of sense and substance. Essentially, the Irish Draught was the all-round horse of the countryside, which could put its hoof to any sort of work and was well able to live rough on economical rations.

The best hunting in the world, and the most expensive, is in the galloping Shire

ABOVE: *A lady rider and horse attack a set of post and rails following the Avon Vale Hunt. The gentleman is less enthusiastic perhaps.*

BELOW: *Italian hunting may not be equal to that enjoyed in Britain, but this member of the Rome Hunt is determined to enjoy his day.*

ABOVE: *For pace, nose and music there is nothing to approach a handsome pack of well-bred English foxhounds.*

LEFT: *A hunt servant in the traditional yellow livery of the Earls of Berkeley. The Berkeley country is one of Britain's largest.*

countries, and with one or two of the top Irish packs. However, it should not be thought that hunting begins and ends with the fashionable hunts. Moreover, it depends what is meant by 'the best'.

There are dozens of hunts (the majority, indeed) that are neither smart nor expensive, in which one can enjoy a full day on a single horse of average ability; the fact that they are situated outside the Shires, and are therefore termed 'provincial', makes no difference at all, and in many the sport shown is very good. However, the right type of horse is essential to make the most of the ground. In the 'plough countries' of East Anglia, a Leicestershire hunter is an embarrassment, and often a nuisance. A good, enduring, short-legged half-bred does the job much better. Similarly, the rough, hilly countries are better suited to an active Welsh Cob, or, if the rider is light enough, a strong pony.

The hunting tradition, as well as packs of hounds, has spread to almost every corner of the world penetrated by the British influence. The British introduced hunting to Spain, Portugal, Italy and the Middle East. It was copied even in Russia, and in altered forms throughout Scandinavia and Asia, most particularly, of course, in India.

In America, however, foxhunting was established at about the time it was taking shape in England, and it has been pursued enthusiastically there ever since.

Hunting in America

American hunting originates in the richly historic states of Virginia, Maryland and Pennsylvania, where the early colonists were quick to establish the sport in the style of the English squirearchy.

Thomas, sixth Earl of Fairfax, was one of the first to own a pack of hounds in the New World. He went to Virginia in 1747, when the country abounded with deer and grey foxes. Red foxes from England were imported early in American history, and became established in the area of Chesapeake Bay. Elsewhere, however, it is the grey fox which provides sport, although neither grey nor red are as plentiful as in England and Ireland. Nor is it customary for American hunts to kill foxes in the numbers that are considered normal and desirable, in the interest of control, in Britain. The organization of the hunt, however, follows the British pattern.

RIGHT: *Hunting in the sunshine at Palm Beach, Florida. American hunts manage to enjoy good sport, although neither the red nor the grey fox is as numerous as in England.*
BELOW: *These hounds are hunting coyote in Arizona with a fair covering of snow.*

Hunt traditions

In England and Ireland, the pack, under the authority of the Masters of Foxhounds Association, is usually the property of a committee, which appoints a Master, or Joint-Masters, to hunt the country and to be responsible for the day-to-day running of the establishment. The committee guarantees the Master, or the Masters, an annual sum to provide sport on a given number of days per week, and from this sum must come the wages of the professional hunt-servants; a huntsman, (or if a Master hunts hounds himself, a kennel-huntsman), assistants – i.e. whippers-in and kennel staff, horses, transport and so on.

The Master is also responsible for appointing a Field-Master, unless, as is more usual, he takes that job himself. The field is subject, in all matters, to the Field-Master's authority.

The huntsman, who is usually, but not always, a professional hunt-servant, is said 'to carry the horn', and he alone hunts the hounds, establishing a rare rapport with his pack. No-one else carries, or would dare to blow, a horn, used by the huntsman to communicate with his hounds, his assistants, the whippers-in, and the field.

The language of hunting may at first sound obscure but is easily enough learnt. Any canine other than a *hound* is a *cur-dog*. Hounds have *sterns* not tails. A pack consists of say 16½ couple of hounds, i.e. 33, and it is *all on* when every hound comprising the pack is present. Hounds are *at fault* when they *check* and cannot *hold* the line. Hounds do not bark, they *speak*, and when they do so on the line of a fox they are said to *throw the tongue*. The *cry* of hounds is the *music*.

Foxes are either *dog-foxes* or *vixen*. Both have a *brush*, four *pads* and a *mask* (face). They live in *earths*, and if they run *straight* to make their *point*, (the distance between the two points of a run), they are called *straight-necked*. A tired fox is referred to as a *sinking* fox. Two foxes are a *brace*, three a *brace and a half*.

'Tally-Ho'? – Well that is pure French, from *Ty a hillaut* or *Il est hault* (he is off).

RIGHT: *The grandeur of hunting is personified in this splendidly apparelled French huntsman.*

HORSES IN COMPETITION

The three Olympic ridden disciplines are dressage, showjumping, and horse-trials, or eventing. Long-distance, or endurance, riding is not yet included in the equestrian Olympics, but it is likely that it will soon take its place with the others.

Every country competing in the equestrian events has its own national championships, and there are continental championships, held in Europe, America and Asia, as well as a World Championship held in the years between the Olympic Games. These, of course, represent competition at the highest level, but none would be possible without the grass roots participation exemplified by competitions, staged at introductory levels, by branches of the Pony Club and the riding club

movement. It is this sort of riding which reflects the modern trend towards keeping horses in urban and suburban conditions, rather than horse-owning being the prerogative of the country dweller.

Apart from racing, the competitive equestrian sports derive almost directly from practical training exercises involved in general military practice.

Even dressage has its roots in warfare, many of the movements being essential accomplishments for a mounted knight. The so-called 'airs above the ground', the leaps of the High School, although probably incomplete and imperfect by the standards of the Spanish School, no doubt acted as an effective deterrent to infantry attempting to attack a single horseman.

All these disciplines, even the more mundane gymkhana games, had their part in military training, but they also served a wider purpose – that of the overall improvement of horse breeds.

In Europe today, breeding policies, outside racing, are almost entirely aligned to the production of competition horses, for the most part purpose-bred for one or other of the major disciplines.

RIGHT: *The immensely impressive and charismatic Milton – probably the greatest, and the most valuable, showjumper in the world. As usual he is ridden by John Whitaker.*
BELOW: *Pony Club mounted games call for a good eye and an intelligent and co-operative pony that knows his job.*

Dressage

Dressage, like so many riding school terms, comes from the French. It derives from the verb *dresser*, which is used to describe the training (or 'dressing') of the riding horse, or even the harness horse.

The discipline has its roots in the progressive system of training described by the Greek general and historian Xenophon (c.430-355 BC). In his books *Hipparchikos* and *Peri Hippikes* he discussed riding as a science and an art. When the riders of the Renaissance began to school their horses in the 'classical' airs, it was to Xenophon that they turned for inspiration. Although he lived over 2,000 years ago, and rode his horses without a saddle and with a relatively straightforward bit, he would recognize at once the collected movements of *piaffe* and *passage*, which are included in the modern Grand Prix Test, and would certainly be familiar with voltes (circles) and serpentines, the riding of which he described so lucidly.

The early classical school was based on the Italian schools at Naples, but, by the time the Spanish Riding School at Vienna had begun in 1572, the Italian influence had diminished, giving way, by the end of the century, to the French schools, which culminated in the École de Versailles and the École de Saumur.

The greatest figure in the advance of educated horsemanship as a rational science was, without doubt, François Robichon de La Guérinière (1688-1751), who was the director of the royal *manège* of the Tuileries between 1730 and 1751.

His teaching, followed in its purest form at the Spanish School, retains its relevance for present-day dressage riders. It was Guérinière who perfected the supreme exercise for suppleness, shoulder-in (*l'épaule en dedans*), as well as head-to-the-wall and tail-to-the-wall – *travers* and *renvers*. He was the first to ride the changes of leg at canter, and he introduced many of the school figures ridden today.

In the nineteenth century, right up to the First World War and beyond, the military riding schools of Europe based their instruction on that of the classical schools. They dominated the equestrian thinking of the day, and it was the 'best-trained charger' tests, devised in the military schools, which were the forerunners of the tests carried out in modern competitive dressage.

Dressage was not included in the Olympic disciplines until the Stockholm Olympics of 1912. There was no team dressage competition, but the Swedes took the first three individual places, and also won the team showjumping and three-day event. In fact, Sweden, then the most advanced of the equestrian countries, repeated that performance at Antwerp in 1920, and headed the dressage line-up in Paris four years later.

The 1912 competition was held in an arena measuring 22×66yds (20×40m), and was at a level that would now be classed as elementary. No lateral movements were

BELOW: *The dressage horse must show freedom in the performance of the extended paces, while remaining submissive to the rider.*

included, no changes of leg in sequence, and, of course, no *piaffe* or *passage*. A jumping test over five fences was, however, part of the competition and this practice persisted in some tests until after the Second World War.

The Antwerp Olympics in 1920 produced a more advanced test. It included counter changes of hand (moving sideways) at trot and canter, and sequence changes of leg at canter up to the one-time changes where the horse changes leading leg every other stride. There was also a system of coefficients for the more difficult movements included in the test.

However, *piaffe* and *passage* were not included in the Olympic test until the 1932 Games at Los Angeles, while canter pirouettes were not performed until the Berlin Games four years later.

As the cavalry became increasingly mechanized, so the military equestrian schools closed one by one and the military influence declined with them. After the Second World War, participation in dressage became almost entirely civilian.

While the classical precepts remained inviolate, dressage moved closer to becoming a sporting discipline, and away from the concept of classical riding as an art-form. Be that as it may, it became the recreation of thousands, and greatly improved the overall understanding of training and riding.

The sport of dressage is divided into grades, with tests ranging from preliminary to advanced level, each nation producing tests suitable for the different standards. Four tests are held at international meetings, and are ridden in an arena measuring 65×197ft (20×60m). The lowest standard of international test is the Prix St. George, followed by intermediates 1 and 2, and then by the Grand Prix, which is the most difficult.

RIGHT: *Warming up in the practice ring at the European Championships, this rider executes a half-pass top the left that is full of energy.*
BELOW: *The most difficult movement of the Grand Prix test is the* piaffe, *which demands a high degree of collection.*

Horse trials

Horse trials, or eventing, also began as military tests. Their object was to test the endurance, speed, stamina and obedience of the horse, as well as the all-round ability of the rider, and they acted as a very clear indicator of the standards of cavalry remount breeding, horse management and horsemanship. The French called these tests *'concours complet'*, the complete test, and it was France that held one of the first events, the *Championat du Cheval d'Armes*, in Paris in 1902. The competition comprised a dressage test, a steeplechase – a 30-mile (48km) race over roads and tracks – and, finally, a jumping test.

The first Olympic Three-Day Event, which was restricted to military riders, was held at the Stockholm Olympics in 1912, and, like the other equestrian competitions, was won by the Swedish team.

The sport remained a purely military affair until after the Second World War, when civilians were allowed to compete, and the sport grew with remarkable speed, female participation becoming increasingly dominant, particularly in Britain.

Probably the greatest single factor in the development of the sport was the establishment of the Badminton Horse Trials, on the Duke of Beaufort's Gloucestershire estate. Badminton, as it became known, first took place in 1949, and, with one or two exceptions due to freak weather conditions, it has been held annually, at the beginning of the year, ever since. It quickly became established as one of the world's most prestigious events, setting standards and becoming a pattern for others staged elsewhere in the world. Obviously, it gave great encouragement to the sport in Britain, contributing largely to the consistent success of the British teams, but it is also regarded internationally as the most important event in the horse-trials calendar, and always attracts its quota of foreign teams and individuals. The trials are always attended by thousands of spectators, whose numbers substantially exceed those found at any other British sporting occasion.

LEFT: *There is no room for hesitation when tackling the complex obstacles at Badminton Horse Trials' famous Lake combination.*

The organization of horse trials is now complex and sophisticated. Horses are graded according to performance records, and there is a carefully devised progression from the pre-novice and novice one-day events to the full-blown three-day championship trials. (In fact, entries are so large that a major horse trial has to be run over four days, two days being devoted to the dressage phase).

In one- and two-day events, the dressage test is held first, followed by showjumping and then the cross-country phase. The three-day event also begins with dressage. The second day is devoted to the speed and endurance phase, central to which is the cross-country course. This latter is preceded by a roads and tracks section, leading to a steeplechase course, after which there is another section of roads and tracks, before the competitors set off on the cross-country. On the final day, after a veterinary examination, there is the showjumping phase, over a comparatively straightforward course, but one that is testing enough after the horse's exertions of the previous day.

The philosophy of the event is that of the early tests for cavalry horses. The dressage test shows that while the horse is at peak fitness it is still able to perform in the confined space of the arena obediently, demonstrating submission to the rider. It is also, of course, a test of supple athleticism. The speed and endurance phase is a test of both those qualities, as well as of the courage and skill of both horse and rider, for the cross-country can contain formidable obstacles. The final showjumping phase confirms that the horse is still sound and 'fit for further service'.

At Badminton, for instance, the endurance phase is over 16 miles (26km), and calls for 1½ hours of sustained effort. The total road and track section is 9½ miles (15km), the steeplechase is 2 miles (3km) and has to be covered in 4½ minutes, at an average speed of about 26mph (40kph). After a 10-minute break there is the 4½ mile (7km) cross-country course with 32 obstacles, many of them combination fences, which means that the horse makes considerably more than 32 jumping efforts.

British and Irish-bred horses generally make the best eventers and are sought after by the riders of both nations. They have a background of hunting, and most will be at least three-quarter or, for preference, seven-eighths Thoroughbred. Such horses have the speed, the mental and physical stamina, the ability, and the courage necessary to tackle this demanding equestrian sport. However, the Thoroughbred is not ideal for dressage, a sport at which the heavier, even-tempered and submissive Warmblood excels.

TOP: *The Whitbread dray obstacle at the Badminton Horse Trials, an event sponsored by the brewery, is big but rarely causes problems for either horse or rider.*
ABOVE: *Immediately before setting out on the cross-country (on the second day of the Trials), competitors have to complete the two-mile steeplechase at racing pace.*

Showjumping

Showjumping is a comparative newcomer to equestrian sport. Since the Second World War, however, with the help of television, it has achieved a spectacular rate of growth to become a major world sport.

Until the end of the nineteenth century, jumping did not figure prominently in the equestrian world. The British and the Irish, of course, jumped in the hunting field, as they had done for a century and a half, but organized arena jumping was unknown.

The first competitions were really held as tests for hunters. In 1865, for instance, the Royal Dublin Society staged a high and wide 'leaping' competition on Leinster Lawn, the first such event to be recorded.

The Paris Show put on a *concours hippique* in the following year, but it did not involve a course of fences erected in an arena. The competitors paraded indoors, but were then sent out into the countryside to jump a course of mostly natural fences.

Jumping was included in the 1900 Paris Olympic Games, when there were three competitions: a timed 'prize jumping', a long jump, and a high jump, but no national team competitions.

Three years later, a very significant event was held at Turin – the first '*Concorso Ippico Internazionale*'. It was confined to the military, but was important because it marked a watershed in riding techniques, as most of the officers concerned, particularly, of course, the Italians, rode in accordance with the forward system introduced and expounded by Captain Federico Caprilli (1868-1907), chief instructor at the cavalry school at Pinerolo. The forward position over fences began to be adopted all over the world from that time, and standards became higher as a result.

Between the two World Wars, international jumping continued in both Europe and America. The International Horse Show at London's Olympia was the backbone of the sport, and staged the first Nations Cup competitions, while in America the National Horse Show at Madison Square Gardens played an increasingly important part.

However, the sport was virtually strangled by its own rules, which were complex, imprecise and varied widely from one country to another. For example, both America and Britain laid thin slats on top of the fences, their dislodgement earning a variety of penalties. Only after the Second

World War, when rules were formulated on an international basis and time became a factor, did the sport really begin to develop.

Once the rules were settled, the popularity of jumping was assured since their uncompromising clarity allowed for a high degree of audience understanding. Today, spectators know the essential rules almost as well as the judges: four for a knockdown, three for a first refusal, six for the second, and elimination for the third. The involvement of time, clearly seen on digital clocks, adds to the excitement, but, above all, enormous strides have been made in course-building at every level, tracks being built with both accuracy and artistry to test the ability of horse and rider.

On the whole, the powerful Warmblood horses of Germany seem to be the dominant influence in showjumping, although in recent years the Selle Français, a wiry horse with quality, courage and ability, has been much in evidence in top international competition.

RIGHT: *Malcolm Pyrah with Towerlands Anglezarke at the 1988 Seoul Olympics.*
BELOW: *Milton, son of Marius, one of the greatest-ever showjumping stallions, makes nothing of a big parallel at Hickstead.*

Distance riding

The sport of distance riding is divided into competitive trail rides and endurance events, the latter being races, held, like all distance rides, under strict veterinary supervision, a matter neglected in many of the military long-distance tests which were the forerunners of the modern sport.

In distance riding no horse exceeds the Arab or its near-derivatives in stamina, endurance and speed.

Hundred-mile rides are held in many countries, and the sport now has its own European and World Championships. In America, which stages over 500 rides each year, the highlight of the season is the famous 100-mile (160km) Western States Ride, known as the Tevis Cup ride, and it is probably the toughest ride of all. First held in 1955, the event runs over the Sierra Nevadas from Tahoe City to Auburn, California. The terrain is formidable, and involves an awesome climb of 9,500ft (2,800m) and temperatures of about 100°F (38°C). For all that, it is usually covered by the leaders in 11-12 hours.

Australia has the Tom Quilty Ride over the same distance, while in Britain the British Open Endurance Riding Championship is the 100-mile (160-km) Summer Solstice Ride, organized by the Endurance Horse and Pony Society. The British Horse Society also organizes 100-milers, the best known being the Golden Horseshoe final, ridden over the rugged Exmoor country. This event is not a race, gold medals being awarded for performances of not less than 8mph (12kph) that incur no penalty points.

LEFT: *The sport of distance riding increases in popularity every year. These riders, competing in Britain's Golden Horseshoe final, have plenty of natural hazards to face.*
BELOW: *High up on Exmoor, Golden Horseshoe riders can make up time on good going.*

INDEX

Picture Credits

Unless otherwise stated, all the
photographs in this book have been
taken by and are the copyright of Bob
Langrish. The publishers wish to thank
the following photographers and
picture agencies who have supplied
other photographs for this book. The
photographs are credited by page
number and position on the page: (B)
Bottom, (T) Top, (C) Centre, (BR)
Bottom right etc.

The Ancient Art and Architecture
Collection: 8, 12, 14(T)

The Anglo-Austrian Society: (Steve
Benbow) 54, 58, 59(B); (The Spanish
Riding School) 55, 60(B), 61(T), 62,
63(R)

Animal Photography Ltd:
(V. Nikiforov) 32; (Sally Anne
Thompson) 11(B), 29, 31

Bruce Coleman: (William S. Paton) 10

Kit Houghton: 78, 79(R), 80(T), 87,
108(C), 115, 119(T)

Only Horses: Front cover, 11(T)

Spectrum Colour Library: 12-3

ZEFA: 81